Alexander Lüdeke

German Heavy Artillery Guns
1933–1945

German Heavy Artillery Guns

1933–1945

Alexander Lüdeke

Pen & Sword
MILITARY

First published in Great Britain in 2015 by
Pen & Sword Military
an imprint of
Pen & Sword Books Ltd
47 Church Street
Barnsley
South Yorkshire
S70 2AS

ISBN 978 1 47382 399 0

A CIP catalogue record for this book is available from the British Library

Typeset in Ehrhardt by
Mac Style Ltd, Bridlington, East Yorkshire
Printed and bound in Malta by Gutenberg Press

Pen & Sword Books Ltd incorporates the imprints of Pen & Sword Archaeology, Atlas,
Aviation, Battleground, Discovery, Family History, History, Maritime, Military, Naval,
Politics, Railways, Select, Transport, True Crime, and Fiction, Frontline Books, Leo Cooper,
Praetorian Press, Seaforth Publishing and Wharncliffe.

For a complete list of Pen & Sword titles please contact
PEN & SWORD BOOKS LIMITED
47 Church Street, Barnsley, South Yorkshire, S70 2AS, England
E-mail: enquiries@pen-and-sword.co.uk
Website: www.pen-and-sword.co.uk

Photo credits: Unless otherwise indicated, all photos come from the author's archive.
Those identified (BA) were published by the Bundesarchiv under a Creative Common
Licence CC by SA 3.0.

Contents

Heavy Field Guns

The 24-cm cannon 3 was the most modern heavy gun of the Wehrmacht but very few of them were manufactured. (Vincent Bourgignion)

The subject of this book is the artillery used between 1933 and 1945 by the German Army, Waffen-SS and Luftwaffe. This first volume handles mortars, infantry, mountain- and light guns as well as anti-tank guns (PAK) and light, medium and heavy field artillery. Flak, railway guns and rockets will be dealt with in a second volume for reasons of space.

When one recalls that the Treaty of Versailles prohibited Germany from having guns with a calibre greater than 7.7-cm from 1919, the broad spectrum of differing gun types which the Wehrmacht had operational only a few years later is amazing. The multitude of guns used was actually greater than that of the USA and USSR for example, who won the war using fewer tried and tested guns.

The German armaments industry, primarily Krupp and Rheinmetall-Borsig, later also Skoda and Böhler, provided an enormous number of competing designs, projects and prototypes but the industry however was never in a position to meet the needs of the troops in artillery. Thus it is not surprising that practically all guns which fell into German hands

Heavy infantry gun 33 (sIG 33) of 15-cm calibre was adopted from 1936 for immediate infantry support. (Holger Erdmann collection).

Glossary	
Flak	Flugabwehrkanone
Gezogenes Rohr	In den Lauf eingefräste »Rillen« (Züge) versetzen das Geschoss beim Abfeuern in Rotation und stabilisieren so dessen Flugbahn.
Glattes Rohr	Lauf ohne Züge, Geschossen werden daher beim Abschuss nicht in Rotation versetzt. Stabilisierung erfolgt meist mittels eines Flossenleitwerks.
GrW	Granatwerfer
HL	Hohlladung
HL-Gr	Hohlladungsgranate
K	Kanone
L/XX	Rohrlänge als Vielfaches des Kalibers, z.B. L/48 für ein 3000 mm langes Rohr des Kalibers 75 mm.
leFH	leichte Feldhaubitze
leGrW	leichter Granatwerfer
leIG	leichtes Infanteriegeschütz
Mündungsbremse	Vorrichtung an der Rohrmündung, welche die dort beim Schuss entweichenden Treibgase so ablenkt, dass der Rückstoß gemindert wird.
NbGr	Nebelgranate
NbWf	Nebelwerfer
Pak	Panzerabwehrkanone
PAW	Panzerabwehrwerfer
PzGr	Panzergranate
RPzB	Raketenpanzerbüchse
Rücklaufsystem	Dient der Dämpfung des Rückstoßes
sFH	schwere Feldhaubitze
sIG	schweres Infanteriegeschütz
sK	schwere Kanone
SK	Schiffkanone
SprGr	Sprenggranate
v0	Mündungsgeschwindigkeit
Vorholer	Mechanische Vorrichtung, die das Rohr nach der Rücklaufphase wieder in die Ausgangsstellung zurückbefördert.
Wgr	Wurfgranate

were kept in service by the Wehrmacht. Often these weapons were only used by occupation troops, coastal artillery or training units but it was not rare for them to be found in use by front troops.

Unfortunately the number of guns used by the Wehrmacht was so great that alongside the series-built types only the most important or technically progressive prototypes and designs can be depicted in this book. The same goes for captured weapons, of which only the most important types find a place,

and those which were modified so fundamentally by the Wehrmacht or industry that the differences between the original German weapon and the foreign one were obliterated.

Until the war's end the guns of the Wehrmacht in general received a designation such as "7.5-cm Pak 40", in this case the 40 indicating the year of introduction or design. Numerous guns introduced in the period from the early to mid-1930s had the number "18" in the designation for reasons of cover

The 15-cm heavy field howitzer 18 (sFH 18, here readied for transport) was the standard Wehrmacht gun of this class throughout the Second World War. (WKA).

(officially the Treaty of Versailles was still in force) to hide the true date of introduction. Captured weapons were given an identification number and in brackets a letter denoting origin, e.g. "7.63-cm field gun 297(r)".

Shortly before the end of the war a new identification system dropped the year figure and instead each weapon was given a number corresponding to the calibre, a letter for the main kind of ammunition used and two figures for the design number of the gun so that for example a field gun developed from the 7.5-cm Pak 40 would have the designation "7M85".

My thanks go to those persons and institutions who kindly allowed me to use their photographs, especial mention here going to Holger Erdmann, Sebastian Hoppe, Paulo Matos (Portugal), Seth Gaines (USA) and Vincent Bourguignon (Belgium). I would also like to thank my life partner Martine Pohl and my son Thore for their support and patience.

5-cm Leichter Granatwerfer 36

Type:	Light mortar
Calibre:	50 mm
Barrel length:	465 mm (L/9.3)
Weight, firing position:	14 kg
Muzzle velocity:	75 m/sec
Weight of bomb:	0.9 kg (Wgr 36)
Traverse:	33°45
Elevation range:	+42°/+90°
Maximum range:	520 m
Rate of fire:	15-25 projectiles/min
Manufacturer:	Developed by Rheinmetall

The development of this smooth bore muzzle-loader began at Rheinmetall in 1934, and reached the troops in 1936. The "light mortar 36" (leGrW 36) was built to facilitate support at the Company level and enable infantry to engage targets beyond the throwing range of hand grenades. With its small size and light weight (14 kg) it could be separated into two parts (baseplate and barrel) and transported by two men. The weapon was expensive to make and until 1938 the models built had a complicated aiming sight. In the course of the war the weapon proved to be too costly, of mediocre performance and not particularly accurate. The range was too short and the bombs not sufficiently effective. Nevertheless up to 1943 over 31,800 leGrW 36 were produced, often lightly modified - thus a number on the Eastern front were given ice spurs for anchorage. The weapon remained operational until the war's end, but front units particularly replaced it with more efficient and accurate captured French or Soviet mortars of the same calibre.

Light mortar 36, notice large baseplate (US Army)

Loading the leGrW 36 (WKA)

8 cm Granatwerfer 34

Type:	Medium mortar
Calibre:	81.4 mm
Barrel length:	1143 mm (L14.1)
Weight for transport:	64 kg (in three parts)
Weight, firing position:	62 kg (steel barrel), 57 kg (light meetal barrel)
Muzzle velocity:	172 m/sec
Weight of bomb:	3.5 kg (Wgr 34)
Traverse:	10° to 23°
Elevation range:	+45°/+90°
Maximum range:	2400 m
Rate of fire:	15–25 rounds/min
Manufacturer:	Developed by Rheinmetall

The GrW 34 was the standard Wehrmacht weapon of this kind at batallion level. Design work began at Rheinmetall in the 1920s, but the troops did not receive it until 1934. It was a smooth muzzle-loader consisting of barrel with closing cap, bipod with traversing and elevating gear, baseplate and aiming sight. At a muzzle velocity of 172 m/sec the 3.5 kg mortar 34 could travel up to 2400 metres. The dispersion at the maximum range was 65 metres. At the outbreak of war the Wehrmacht had over 3625 GrW 34's: by March 1945 73,000 had been turned out. Mounted on self-propelled chassis the weapon became the "GrW 67" or "GrW 34/1". It earned for itself the reputation of great accuracy and rate of fire, but that had probably less to do with its design than the excellent training of its crews. A lighter version with shorter barrel (L/9.2) originally developed for the paratroop arm was designated "GrW 42". It was complemented by numerous captured 81.4-mm mortars from practically all occupied European countries and Soviet 82-mm mortars.

Loading the 8-cm Grw 34 (US Army)

The 8-cm Grw 34 was the standard medium-mortar of the Wehrmacht. (US Army)

8, 14-cm Granatwerfer 278(f)

Type:	Medium mortar
Calibre:	81.4 mm
Barrel length:	11267 mm (L/15.6)
Weight for transport:	59.7 kg
Weight, firing position:	59.7 kg
Muzzle velocity:	174 m/sec
Weight of bomb:	3.25 kg (light Wgr), 6.5 kg (heavy Wgr)
Traverse:	8°-12°
Elevation range:	+45°/+85°
Maximum range:	2850 m (light Wgr), 1200 m (heavy Wgr)
Rate of fire:	Up to 20 rounds/min
Manufacturer:	Developed by Brandt, Paris

In 1927 Edgar Brandt designed this weapon as an improvement of the British Stokes model from the First World War and created what is practically the ancestor of all modern mortars. The mortar, called "Mortier Brandt mle 27/31" by the French Army, had a calibre of 81.4 mm and was a simple smooth bore weapon loaded through the muzzle. Baseplate, bipod, gunsight, traverse and elevating gear weighed 59.7 kg and could be disassembled into three parts. The basics of Brandt's design can be seen even today in modern systems: it represents a milestone in weapons history. It is therefore no surprise that this weapon was exported to numerous countries during the 1930s or made in them under licence.

The 8.14-cm Brandt mortar was practically the ancestor of all modern weapons of this kind. (Vincent Bourguignon)

After the fall of France in the summer of 1940 the Wehrmacht seized all available Brandt mortars and commissioned them, as according to the version, as "8.14-cm Granatwerfer 278(f)" or "278/1(f)". In addition large numbers of these weapons fell into German hands in Austria, Czechoslovakia, Poland, Denmark, Holland and Yugoslavia. Although there were some differences between the various models, the ammunition was interchangeable, so that munition stocks could be used with all models without a problem. The Wehrmacht used Brandt mortars of Austrian and Czech origin from the outbreak of war.

10-cm Nebelwerfer 35

Type:	Medium mortar
Calibre:	105 mm
Barrel length:	1344 mm (L/13)
Weight for transport:	110 kg (in three parts)
Weight, firing position:	105 kg
Muzzle velocity:	193 m/sec
Weight of bomb:	7.38 kg (Wgr 35)
Traverse:	28°
Elevation range:	+45°/+90
Maximum range:	3025 m
Rate of fire:	10-15 rounds/min
Manufacturer:	developed by Rheinmetall

The "Nebelwerfer 35" (NbWf 35) was intended to fire only smoke or gas ammunition, but could be used for conventional HE mortar bombs. Its development began in 1934, but the first mortars were not built until 1939 and supplied to smoke-units. The NbWf 35 was basically a larger version of the GrW 34, which it closely resembled. The weapon could be dismantled into three parts for transport. The weight of the individual elements (baseplate 36.3 kg, barrel 31.7 kg and tripod 32.2 kg) was unfavourable for manual handling over long stretches and the crew had a small hand cart for transporting it. A range of 3025 metres was possible with a muzzle velocity of 193 m/sec. Scatter at the extreme limit was 65 m. Only 627 NbWf 35 had been manufactured when a halt was called to production in May 1941. The rocket launchers "10-cm NbWf 40" and "15-cm NbWf 41" succeeded it.

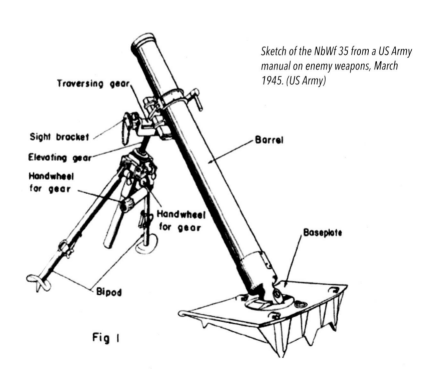

Sketch of the NbWf 35 from a US Army manual on enemy weapons, March 1945. (US Army)

Traversing gear

Sight bracket

Elevating gear

Handwheel for gear

Barrel

Handwheel for gear

Baseplate

Bipod

Fig I

10-cm Nebelwerfer 40

Type:	Medium mortar
Calibre:	105 mm
Barrel length:	1858 mm (L17.7)
Weight for transport:	892 kg
Weight, firing position:	800 kg
Muzzle velocity:	310 m/sec
Weight of bomb:	8.65 kg (Wgr 40), 8.9 kg (smoke bomb)
Traverse:	14°
Elevation range:	+45°/+84°
Maximum range:	6300 m
Rate of fire:	8–10 rounds/min
Manufacturer:	Developed by Rheinmetall

In 1937 the Army wanted a successor to the (not yet introduced) NbWf 35 with greater range and accuracy. Rheinmetall then developed two very similar mortars (NbWf 51 and 52) which went no further than trials with the units but became the design basis for the "NbWf 40". Although smooth bore as other mortars, it was a rear-loader with barrel recoil suppression system and an integral wheeled chassis. Because the mortar was fired while on this chassis, at first sight it looked like a gun. The NbWf 40 had a longer barrel than the NbWf 35 and could fire a somewhat heavier bomb more then twice the distance. It was a much more complicated weapon and more expensive to produce. Its weight was only approximately eight times that of the NbWf 35, but instead of 1500 Reichsmarks it was marketed at 14,000 Reichsmarks.

The first NbWf 40 were delivered to the smoke troops at the end of 1940. Because work on the

NbWf 40 of the Luftwaffe Field Division Hermann Göring on manouevres in the Reich. (BA)

"15-cm NbWf 41" rocket launcher began shortly after, production of the NbWf 40 was cut back and by the end of 1943 only 317 of them had been turned out.

The NbWF 40 as depicted in a 1945 US Army manual. (US Army)

12-cm
Granatwerfer 42

After the attack on the Soviet Union in the summer of 1941, the Wehrmacht captured gigantic quantities of Soviet war material including an imposing number of 120-mm mortars. This conventionally-built smooth bore muzzle loader was a copy of the French "Mortier Brandt de 120-mm modèle 1935" and had been introduced into the Red Army under the designation "M1938" in 1939. The 285 kg mortar was transported dismantled into three parts (barrel, tripod and baseplate), but also came with a skilfully designed single-axle trailer which could be quickly attached to the baseplate ready to tow.

The Wehrmacht was so impressed by the hitting power, mobility and simplicity of the captured models that they copied the Soviet weapon. Built by

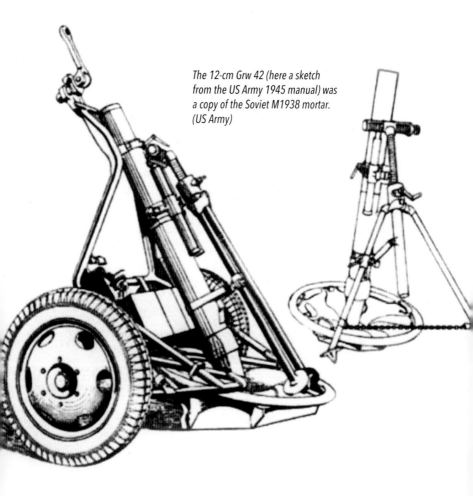

The 12-cm Grw 42 (here a sketch from the US Army 1945 manual) was a copy of the Soviet M1938 mortar. (US Army)

the Brünner Maschinenfabrik, slightly improved examples were designated "Granatwerfer 42", the Soviet original as "12-cm Granatwerfer 378(r)". The German version could fire both Soviet and German ammunition to a range of 6050 metres, the Soviet version had a maximum range of 5700 metres. While the Soviets considered the mortar to be an artillery piece, the Wehrmacht used it at once to support the infantry, and the GrW 42 occasionally replaced infantry guns. By the war's end around 8500 GrW 42 had been produced. Together with the Soviet original, the GrW 42 was one of the best mortars of the war.

Type:	Medium mortar
Calibre:	120 mm
Barrel length:	1865 mm (L15.5)
Weight for transport:	560 kg (with transport-chassis)
Weight, firing position:	285 kg
Muzzle velocity:	283 m/sec
Weight of bomb:	15.6 kg (Wgr 42)
Traverse:	16°
Elevation range:	+45°/+84°
Maximum range:	6050 m
Rate of fire:	6–10 rounds/min
Manufacturer:	Erste Brünner Maschinenfabrik

A 12-cm Granatwerfer M1938 abandoned by the Red Army, redesignated "12-cm GrW 378(r)" by the Wehrmacht. Notice the ammunition trailer at the right.

20-cm leichter Ladungswerfer

Type:	Light grenade-launcher
Calibre:	Diameter of firing tube 90 mm
Barrel length:	540 mm firing tube
Weight, firing position:	93 kg
Muzzle velocity:	88 m/sec
Weight of projectile:	21.27 kg (Wgr 40)
Traverse:	5°
Elevation range:	+45°/+80°
Maximum range:	700 m
Rate of fire:	Maximum 8 projectiles/min
Manufacturer:	Rheinmetall

At first glance this weapon looked like a conventional mortar but instead of a barrel had a 540-mm long firing tube. Into this tube the hollow shaft of a fin-stabilized large-headed grenade would drop and detonate upon electrical contact with the lower end of the tube. The weapon was used primarily by assault pioneers for firing explosive rounds to bring down field fortifications, but also for smoke rounds and so-called "harpoon rounds". The latter had a rope with numerous explosive charges attached for clearing a way through a minefield. The weapon developed in 1939 at Rheinmetall was adopted in April 1940 and used on the Western Front in May

and June that year. On the whole the weapon proved itself. Rheinmetall built only 158 of them, and after 1942 they were withdrawn from the front. Less than that number of the large version (38-cm heavy grenade launcher) were built, being found far too heavy and cumbersome (weight for firing 1600 kg).

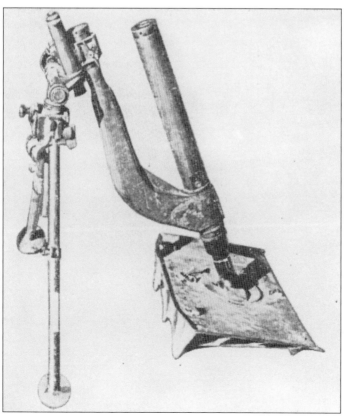

The light grenade-launcher was used primarily by assault pioneers (US Army).

21-cm Granatwerfer 69

Type:	Heavy mortar
Calibre:	210.9 mm
Barrel length:	3000 mm (L/14.2)
Weight for transport:	2800 kg
Weight, firing position:	2800 kg
Muzzle velocity:	285 m/sec (light Wgr), 247 m/sec (heavy Wgr)
Weight of bomb:	80 kg (light Wgr), 110 kg (heavy Wgr)
Traverse:	60°
Elevation range:	+45°/+75°
Maximum range:	6300 m (light Wgr), 5190 m (heavy Wgr)
Rate of fire:	1-2 rounds/min
Manufacturer:	Skoda Works

In the search for a simple, mobile and economic but yet powerful weapon, in 1944 the Wehrmacht turned to Skoda at Pilsen. Skoda had designed a 22-cm heavy mortar designated "B14" which the Wehrmacht wanted modified to 21-cm. The first protoype was introduced and accepted by the Wehrmacht in August 1944 as "GrW 69". It was a rear-loader with a massive recoil and fitted to a two-wheel chassis on which it fired. A ball-and-socket joint at the baseplate enabled the mortar to be traversed. Beforehand a 6-metre surface had to be levelled to lay a small railed track. The wheels of the mortar chassis ran along this track by means of a waggon mount. The GrW 69 could only fire in the upper register groups, elevation being achieved with the aid of two lateral ratcheted-poles. For loading, the barrel had to be in an almost horizontal position. The first GrW 69's reached the front in November 1944, the exact number produced up to May 1945 being unknown but it must have been well below 200.

21-cm Grw 69 in the artillery museum at Fort Sill, USA (Jason Long, cc by sa 3.0)

7.5-cm leichtes Infanterie-geschütz 18

The Reichswehr received this gun (leIG 18) at the beginning of the 1930s as an immediate infantry support weapon independent of the divisional artillery. The Rheinmetall design had a breech mechanism "like a rifle" and a simple box tail chassis with wooden wheels for horse haulage. From 1937 steel wheels with all-rubber tyres were also manufactured.

In 1935 a mountain warfare version with a lighter chassis (leGebIG 18) was designed which could be rapidly disassembled into ten parts. Although intended only as an interim solution until the

Type:	Light infantry gun
Calibre:	75 mm
Barrel length:	885 mm (L11.8)
Weight for transport:	405 kg (horse-drawn)
	515 kg (motor drawn)
Weight, firing position:	400 kg (horse-drawn),
	570 kg (motor drawn)
Muzzle velocity:	221 m/sec
Weight of shell:	6 kg (Inf-Gr 18)
Traverse:	11°
Elevation range:	–10°/+75°
Maximum range:	3550 m (with supplementary
	charge, 4600 m)
Rate of fire:	8 to 12 rounds/min
Manufacturer:	Developed by Rheinmetall,
	Düsseldorf

A horse-drawn 7.5-cm leIG 18, wheels with wooden spokes, on manouevres in Pomerania, late summer 1938 (WKA)

introduction of the planned Geb 36, this gun remain operational until 1945. Only eight units of the leIG 18F for the paratroop arm were built, the later mid-1930s development designated 7.5-cm IG L/13 went no further than the experimental stage.

The leIG 18 was one of the most ubiquitous Wehrmacht guns. There were 2933 on hand when the war began and up to May 1945 a total of almost 12,000 leIG 18 and leGebIG 18 had been produced.

7.5-cm leIG 18 during gunnery training. (Holger Erdmann collection)

Training on the leIG 18. (Holger Erdmann collection)

7.5-cm Infanteriegeschütz 42 und 37

In 1940 the Heereswaffenamt (Army Weapons Department) was looking for a modern infantry gun. Krupp then developed its "IG 42" which proceeded no further than the prototype. Not until 1944 was this design revived and given a new chassis (which was also used for the 8-cm PAW 600 (anti-tank launcher). A characteristic of the new IG 42 in particular was the large four- chamber deflector muzzle brake (which diverted the propellant gases so as to reduce recoil). Of the 1450 IG 42 wanted, only a few more than 500 reached the troops. At the end of 1944 the IG-42 barrel was combined with the old chassis of the "German 3.7-cm Pak 36" or the "3.7-cm Beute-Pak 158(r)" to make the "Pak 37" anti-tank gun, later designated "IG 37". The 7.5-cm hollow charge shell of the IG 37 would penetrate up to 85 mm of armour at combat range. A total of almost 2300 IG 37 were built of which more than 1300 were still with the fighting troops at the war's end.

Below and right: IG 37 in the Panzermuseum, Munster. (Sebastian Hoppe)

Type:	Infantry gun
Calibre:	75 mm
Barrel length:	885 mm (L/22.4)
Weight for transport:	530 kg
Weight, firing position:	510 kg
Muzzle velocity:	280 m/sec (hollow charge shell 385 m/sec)
Weight of shell:	5.45 kg (Inf-Gr 38)
Traverse:	58°
Elevation range:	–10°/+40°
Maximum range:	5150 m
Rate of fire:	8–12 rounds/min
Manufacturer:	Developed by Krupp, Essen (barrel) and Rheinmetall, Düsseldorf (chassis).

Illustration of the IG 37 in a US Army handbook. (US Army)

15-cm schweres Infanteriegeschütz 33

Type:	Heavy infantry gun
Calibre:	149.1 mm
Barrel length:	1163 mm (L/11.4)
Weight for transport:	1700 kg (horse-drawn), 1825 kg (drawn by motor vehicle)
Weight, firing position:	1680 kg (horse-drawn), 1800 kg (drawn by motor vehicle)
Muzzle velocity:	240 m/sec (Infanterie-Gr 33)
Weight of shell:	38 kg (Infanterie-Gr 33)
Traverse:	11°
Elevation range:	-4°/+75°
Maximum range:	4700 m
Rate of fire:	2-3 rounds/min
Manufacturer:	Developed by Rheinmetall, Düsseldorf

In 1927 Rheinmetall embarked upon several studies for a heavy infantry gun which resulted finally in 1933 in the design for a 15-cm gun with box tail chassis. The gun, designated "sIG 33", entered series production in 1936. Although the sIG 33 proved robust and powerful, it was too heavy and unmanageable as an infantry support weapon. In 1938 therefore the weight of the chassis was reduced by the partial use of light metals. Because this material was scarce and reserved for aircraft production, only a few of the lighter guns (Modell B) were so made. Early examples were horse-drawn, those coming later had steel wheels with all-rubber tyres. The sIG 38 fired heavy HE as well as hollow charge and smoke shells. From 1942 for assaults on field fortifications a 300 mm grenade with haft was introduced weighing 90 kg and containing 27 kg of

HE. At the outbreak of war the Wehrmacht had over 410 sIG 33, and up to 1945 a total of 4565 were produced.

15-cm sIG 33 with rubber tyres for motorized transport, horse-drawn sIG 33 had steel rims. (US Army)

Side profile of the sIG 33 with maximum elevation of the barrel. (Holger Erdmann collection)

15-cm sIG with improvised winter camouflage. (Holger Erdmann collection).

7.62-cm Infanteriekanonenh aubitze 290(r)

This weapon with box tail chassis was developed in 1927 for the regimental artillery units of the Red Army and built between 1928 and 1943. At the beginning of the campaign on the Eastern Front the Soviet Army had 4708 of these guns, and by the time when production was halted in 1943, a total of 16,482 had been manufactured. Early examples of the "7.6-cm Regimentskanone Modell 1927" as originally designated had wheels with wooden spokes, later some of steel with rubber tyres more suitable for motor traction.

During the opening phase of the Eastern campaign the Wehrmacht captured thousands of examples of this simple but robust artillery and used them under the designation "7.62-cm Infanteriekanonenhaubitze 290(r)" as infantry guns. The weapon was available in such large numbers (at end of 1943 there were 1815 guns on hand) and so highly thought of that they were given German optics while German ammunition (HE and hollow charge shells) was manufactured to suit.

Type:	Infantry gun
Calibre:	76.2 mm
Barrel length:	1250 mm (L16/5)
Weight for transport:	1595 kg (with limber)
Weight, firing position:	780 kg
Muzzle velocity:	387 m/sec
Weight of shell:	6.4 kg (HE)
Traverse:	6°
Elevation range:	–6°/+25°
Maximum range:	8850 m
Rate of fire:	14 rounds/min
Manufacturer:	USSR

Winter on the Eastern front, an Infanteriekanonenhaubitze 290(r) under tow by a Wehrmacht armoured vehicle.

62-cm Infanteriekanonen haubitze 290(r) in the museum at Drzonov, Poland.

7.5-cm Gebirgskanone 15

Type:	Mountain gun
Calibre:	75 mm
Barrel length:	1155 mm (L15/4)
Weight for transport:	613 kg
Weight, firing position:	613 kg
Muzzle velocity:	349 m/sec
Weight of shell:	6.35 kg (HE)
Traverse:	7°
Elevation range:	-10°/+50°
Maximum range:	6650 m
Rate of fire:	6–8 rounds/min
Manufacturer:	Skoda Works, Pilsen

This Skoda development was used by the Austro-Hungarian Army as "M1915" at the beginning of the First World War while a few of the guns went to the German Reich. Typically for a mountain gun, this design with box tail carriage and wooden-spoked wheels could be dismantled rapidly into six (or seven if one counts the splinter shield) parts weighing between 78 kg and 156 kg each for transport by mule. After 1918 they were retained by the successor States to the Hapsburg Empire (and some given to Italy as reparations),and in 1938/39 a number of these guns fell into the hands of the Wehrmacht at the annexation of Austria and the occupation of Czechoslovakia, and used as German mountain guns to make up the shortage. Although only an interim solution (designation "GebK 15") awaiting the introduction of the planned Gebirgsgeschütz 36, these old guns remained in service until 1945. Those taken over from the Italians after 1943 were designated "GebK 259(i)".

7.5-cm Gebirgskanone 15 in the Athens War Museum. (Konstantinos Stampoulis)

7.5-cm Gebirgshaubitze 34

Type:	Mountain gun
Calibre:	75 mm
Barrel length:	1800 mm (L/24)
Weight for transport:	928 kg
Weight, firing position:	928 kg
Muzzle velocity:	455 m/sec
Weight of shell:	6.59 kg (HE)
Traverse:	7.5°
Elevation range:	–10°/+50°
Maximum range:	9300 m
Rate of fire:	Not known
Manufacturer:	AB Bofors, Karlskoga (Sweden)

Because of its lack of mountain guns, it is supposed that in the mid-1930s the Wehrmacht bought twelve howitzers of this type in Sweden. This "Gebirgshaubitze 34" (based on Krupp plans of the 1920s) was produced by the armaments manufacturer Bofors which sold them to Belgium, China and Argentina amongst others. In 1940 the Wehrmacht captured practically all 20 (or depending on source, 24) Belgian "Canon de 75 mle 1934" which then became "Gebirgskanone 228(b)". The Belgians had not used them as mountain howitzers but as infantry guns with slightly modified chassis and pneumatic tyres. The howitzer could be disassembled swiftly into eight parts. The mountain troops tried placing GebH 34 on some RSG (Raupenschlepper Gebirge-crawler tractors for mountains, a modified version of the Raupenschlepper Ost) to make a self-propelled chassis, but this did not prove successful.

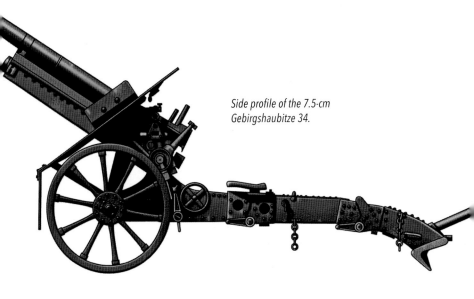

Side profile of the 7.5-cm Gebirgshaubitze 34.

7.5-cm Gebirgsgeschütz 36

Type:	Mountain gun
Calibre:	75 mm
Barrel length:	1450 mm (L/19.5)
Weight for transport:	750 kg
Weight, firing position:	750 kg
Muzzle velocity:	475 m/sec
Weight of shell:	5.83 kg (HE)
Traverse:	40°
Elevation range:	-2°/+70°
Maximum range:	9250 m
Rate of fire:	6–8 rounds/min
Manufacturer:	Developed by Rheinmetall, built by Wolf, Magdeburg

Although Rheinmetall had begun designing new 7.5-cm and 10.5-cm mountain guns in 1926, it was not until 1935 that the Army Weapons Department accepted a submission for a 7.5-cm gun. GebG 36 was complete by 1938 and but not delivered to the troops until 1940. By 1945 a total of 1193 units had been produced. Some of the earlier examples still had wheels with wooden spokes, later models were given metal wheels with rubber tyres capable of being replaced by skis for work in snow. The chassis tail spread into two parts for stability when shooting, and the gun could be dismantled into eight parts for transport. The large cylindrical mouth brake, the absence of the splinter shield and massive baseplate were noticeable. Although the GebG 36 proved successful and became the standard gun of the mountain artillery, when firing over a flat trajectory it tended to "buck". Using the major propellants it was therefore forbidden to fire with a barrel elevation of less than 15°, otherwise the GebG36 "leapt" upwards. Steep trajectory fire was no problem for then the ground absorbed a large part of the recoil force.

7.5-cm mountain gun 36, notice the cylindrical "pepper-pot muzzle brake" (US Army)

GebG 36 under tow by an Sd.Kfz 2 (crawler-type motor cycle).

Illustration of the GenG 36 from a US Army handbook. (US Army)

GERMAN 75-MM
MOUNTAIN GUN

10.5-cm Gebirgshaubitze 40

Besides a 7.5-cm weapon for the mountain troops the Army Weapons Department also wanted a 10.5-cm howitzer, as a result of which two prototypes of this calibre from Rheinmetall and Böhler were tested in 1940, the latter being chosen. The Böhler gun included a series of noteworthy innovations. Thus for example when the chassis tail was splayed the wheels lifted so that the lower chassis rested on a

Dachsteingebirge, Upper Danube: mountain troops at a 10.5-cm GebH 40 in firing position. (BA)

Type:	Mountain gun
Calibre:	105 mm
Barrel length:	3150 mm (L/30)
Weight for transport:	2600 kg (four sections)
Weight, firing position:	1656 kg
Muzzle velocity:	570 m/sec
Weight of shell:	14.81 kg (HE)
Traverse:	50°
Elevation range:	–5°/+70°
Maximum range:	12,625 m
Rate of fire:	4-6 rolunds/min
Manufacturer:	Gebr. Böhler, Kopfenberg

central firing platform. The GebH 40 could be dismantled into five parts for transport, of which four would be loaded on a single-axle trailer. The fifth was the lower chassis which ran on its own wheels. These weights (680 to 720 kg each) were drawn by an Sd.Kfz.2 (NSU crawler motor cycle combination). The gun could also be drawn intact. Although very heavy, the GebH 40 was very efficient and it numbers amongst the best of the mountain guns ever built. Between 1942 and 1945 the firm Gebrüder Böhler of Kapfenberg/Styria/Austria built 420 howitzers of this type.

Notice the small chassis of the GebH 40 in comparison to the barrel length. (US Army).

7.5-cm Gebirgshaubitze 254(i)

This weapon was developed originally by the armaments firm Ansaldo and introduced into the Italian Army as "Obice da 75/18 Modello 34" in 1934. Provided with a box tail carriage, rubber-tyred wheels with steel spokes and a characteristic frame-

7.5-cm Gebirgshaubitze 254(i)
exhibited at Heraclion, Crete. (PD)

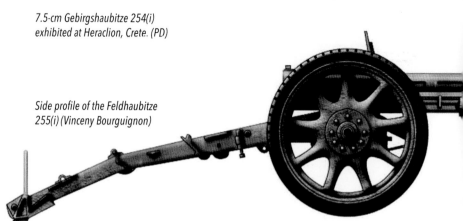

Side profile of the Feldhaubitze
255(i) (Vinceny Bourguignon)

Type:	Mountain gun
Calibre:	75 mm
Barrel length:	1557 mm (L/20.8)
Weight for transport:	820 kg
Weight, firing position:	780 kg
Muzzle velocity:	425 m/sec
Weight of shell:	6.4 kg (HE)
Traverse:	40°
Elevation range:	–10°/+65°
Maximum range:	9560 m
Rate of fire:	6–8 rounds/min
Manufacturer:	Ansaldo, Pozzuoli

like barrel cradle, it could be dismantled into eight parts. For standardization purposes and simplification of ammunition supply the barrel was fitted on a simplified field chassis intended for motor traction. After these modifications the light howitzer was redesignated "Obice da 75/18 Modello 35". Both variants of this weapon were equally efficient as modern guns and formed the backbone of the Italian artillery. After September 1943 the Wehrmacht took charge of all examples it could find and used them until the capitulation as "Gebirgshaubitze 254(i)" and also "Feldhaubitze 255(i)".

One of the "7.5-cm Obice da 75/18 modello 34" used by the Portuguese Army until the 1960s, taken at Evora-Alentejo, "Comando de Instruçao e Doutrina do Exército" (Portugal). Notice the folded-up chassis tail. (Paulo Matos)

7.5-cm Leichtgeschütz 40

Type:	Recoil-free gun
Calibre:	75 mm
Barrel length:	750 mm (L/10)
Weight for transport:	212 kg
Weight, firing position:	207 kg (145 kg without wheels)
Muzzle velocity:	345 m/sec
Weight of shell:	5.83 kg (HE)
Traverse:	360° (under 20° and above 50° elevation)
Elevation range:	–15°/+65°
Maximum range:	6500 m
Rate of fire:	6–8 rounds/min
Manufacturer:	Rheinmetall, Düsseldorf; Dürrkopp, Bielefeld.

Recoil-free guns were designated "Leichtgeschütze" (LG) in Germany. The gases released at detonation streamed out of the barrel rear to neutralize the recoil. This principle allowed a very light chassis. A decisive disadvantage, however, was that the gases betrayed the position of the gun. Additionally the powder required was substantially higher than for conventional guns because only 20% of the charge was used to propel the shell. Development began at Rheinmetall in 1937, the delivery of light gun LG 1, which could be landed from the air, followed in 1940. After improvements to the chassis (amongst others a tripod for a traverse of 360°) and breech it was re-designated "LG 40". For parachute drops the LG 40 could be separated into four, later two parts. It received its baptism of fire (also used by mountain troops) in the conquest of Crete in May 1941. A total of 450 units had been built by 1944, 180 at Rheinmetall, Düsseldorf and 270 at Dürrkopf, Bielefeld.

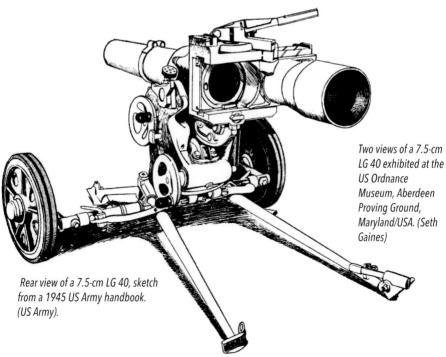

Two views of a 7.5-cm LG 40 exhibited at the US Ordnance Museum, Aberdeen Proving Ground, Maryland/USA. (Seth Gaines)

Rear view of a 7.5-cm LG 40, sketch from a 1945 US Army handbook. (US Army).

10.5-cm Leichtgeschütz 40

Type:	Recoil-free gun
Calibre:	105 mm
Barrel length:	1380 mm (L/13)
Weight for transport:	476 kg
Weight, firing position:	431 kg
Muzzle velocity:	380 m/sec
Weight of shell:	14.74 kg (HE)
Traverse:	80°
Elevation range:	–15°/+42°
Maximum range:	8000 m
Rate of fire:	6–7 rounds/min
Manufacturer:	Krupp, Essen

After the 7.5-cm light gun had proved itself, the paratroop arm wanted a larger calibre weapon. Krupp and Rheinmetall therefore submitted competing guns in 1942 of which the Krupp version was ready for the front earlier. The design had a short box chassis with spurs and two all-rubber- tyred wheels which could be removed for firing. The large Laval jet was swivelled aside during loading. It had been observed on the 7.5-cm light gun that the light construction could distort because of the shell spin in the barrel. Therefore Krupp inserted into the gas exhaust jet of its gun three "wings" (counter-spin blades) which counter-acted the gas flow of the rotation.

For a parachute drop the weapon could be dismantled into five parts, below the muzzle was a lug for towing. The "LG 40" fired leFH 18 shells of the same calibre. The chassis of the LG 40 consisted initially of aluminium and magnesium (LG 40/1). Because of the wartime shortage of light metals, production changed over to steel (LG 40/2). Output ceased in 1944, the exact number of this type made by Krupp is not known

10.5-cm LG 40 of a paratroop unit, San Felice (Italy), December 1943. (BA)

10.5-cm Leichtgeschütz 40 with missing tyres, probably battle damage. (US Army)

10.5-cm Leichtgeschütz 42

Type:	Recoil-free gun
Calibre:	105 mm
Barrel length:	1374 mm (L13/.1)
Weight for transport:	550 kg
Weight, firing position:	490 kg
Muzzle velocity:	380 m/sec
Weight of shell:	14.74 kg (HE)
Traverse:	360° (below 12°, above 70° barrel elevation).
Elevation range:	–15°/+42°
Maximum range:	8000 m
Rate of fire:	6–7 rounds/min
Manufacturer:	Rheinmetall, Dürkopp.

The "LG 42" was Rheinmetall's answer to the request by the paratroop arm for a heavier gun. Its ballistic achievement was similar to that of the Krupp design, the ammunition being similar. Rheinmetall copied from the LG 40 the idea of the counter-spin blades. Outwardly however the two weapons were clearly different. The LG 42 (like the 7.5-cm LG 40) had a tripod chassis with axle for two detachable wheels with all-rubber tyres. For transport the leading leg was attached under the barrel, the rear two folded as a conventional box tail pair. Chassis production switched over to steel during the war for the scarcity of light metals (LG 42/1 and LG 42/2). Up to 1944 a total of 528 units of the two 10.5-cm light guns (Krupp LG 40 and Rheinmetall LG 42) were produced, probably the majority of them coming from Rheinmetall. The Rheinmetall "LG 43" was the LG 42 with improved chassis, but few were built.

10.5-cm LG 42/1 with light metal chassis. (US Army)

Panzerfaust Modelle 30, 60, 100 and 150

Although it may not appear to be so at first glance, the Panzerfaust in all its variants was a recoil-free gun. A large-calibre hollow charge grenade was placed at the head of a thin-walled barrel, (provided with its powder charge at the works). When fired the warhead was stabilized in flight by fins which folded outwards. As usual with light guns, the gas flow from the detonation escaping at the barrel end compensated for the recoil, but was dangerous to anybody standing near the rear end and also betrayed the position of the shooter.

From mid-1942 the Hugo Schneider AG (HASAG) works at Leipzig began the development of a one-man anti-tank weapon, the "Faustpatrone". This weapon provided the basic principle for the later Panzerfaust, but had a warhead of less rounded form which often slid off slanting armour. Early examples also had no aiming sight. The first of these weapons

("Faustpatrone klein, 30 m") could penetrate 140 mm steel armour and were delivered in August 1943. Because of the mentioned tendency to be deflected without effect by slanting armour surfaces, after the first tests an improved version was forthcoming equipped with a simple sight and a rounded, more favourably shaped warhead containing double the explosive (0.8 kg instad of 0.4 kg) which could go through 200 mm steel armour. Despite almost double the powder charge (100 grams instead of 54 grams) the range remained the same because of the size and weight of the warhead, and so the weapon was known as "Panzerfaust 30". The first examples of these were also delivered in August 1943.

"Panzerfaust 60" entered production in September 1944. Whereas the warhead itself remained unmodified, the range was increased to 60 metres by raising the powder charge to 134 grams. This was the most produced of the Panzerfaust variants. To increase the range farther to 100 metres, in November 1944 the powder charge was increased to 200 grams, this variant being known as "Panzerfaust 100". Shortly before the war's end a few models of the "Panzerfaust 150" (range 150 m) reached the fronts: this variant had been thoroughly worked over

Panzerfaust 100 at a weapons exhibition at Chino, California. Behind it is a Panzerbüchse 54.

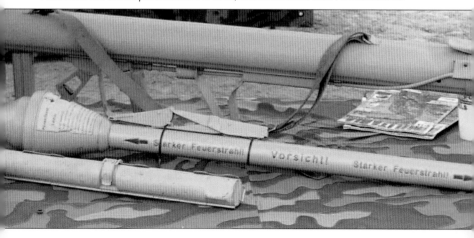

Type:			Recoil free gun		
Designation:	Faust patrone	Pzfst	Pzfst	Pzfst	Pzfst
	Small, 30 m	30 m	60m	100m	150m
Weapon length:	98.5 cm	104.5	104.5	115	Not known
Total weight:	3.2 kg	5.1kg	6.1kg	6.8kg	6.5 kg
Weight of propellant:	54 gms	100gm	134gm	200gm	200gm
Weight of hollow charge:	400 gms	800kg	800kg	800kg	Not known
Barrel diameter:	32 mm	44mm	50mm	60mm	Not known
Warhead diameter:	100 mm	149mm	149mm	149mm	Not known
Muzzle velocity:	28 m/sec	30m/s	45 m/s	60 m/s	85 m/s
Effective range:	30 m	30m	60m	100m	150m
Penetrative power:	140 mm/90°	*200 mm/90°	*200 mm/90°	*200 mm/90°	300mm/90°

Top group: "Use of the Panzerfaust" (t.left) Remove safety wire (t.right) Raise sight (b.left) Put safety lever to "unlocked" (b.right) If you now press the catch which says Fire, the warhead will be discharged.

Instructions for using the Panzerfaust from a Wehrmacht handbook.

Bottom group: Firing stances for the Panzerfaust

and now had a conical 106-mm calibre head giving improved penetration, and a reloadable tube. In order to increase effectiveness against unarmoured targets, a so-called "splinter-ring" could be added. The "Panzerfaust 250" was to have had a muzzle velocity of 150 m/sec, a pistol grip and a rear-loadable tube, but never got beyond the project study stage.

The exact number of all Panzerfaust produced at HASAG and by other firms cannot be established, but it must have been several million. The Panzerfaust was also used by Axis allies of the Wehrmacht such as Finland.

Waiting for the attack: soldiers in a trench with a Panzerfaust 60.

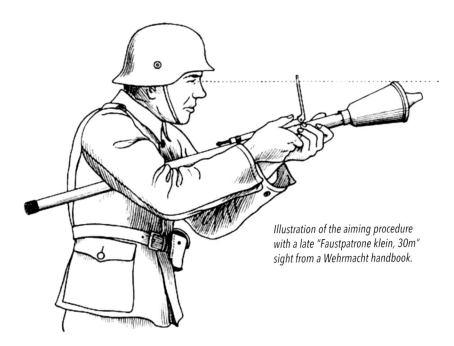

Illustration of the aiming procedure with a late "Faustpatrone klein, 30m" sight from a Wehrmacht handbook.

Volkssturm men in Berlin armed with the Panzerfaust, April 1945. (BA)

2.8-cm schwere Panzerbüchse 41

Type:	Light Pak
Calibre:	28/20 mm
Barrel length:	1714 mm (L/61.2)
Weight for transport:	229 kg
Weight, firing position:	229 kg
Muzzle velocity:	1400 m/sec
Weight of shell:	0.131 kg (armour shell), 0085 kg (HE)
Traverse:	90° (at 0° elevation)
Elevation range:	–5°/+45°
Effective range:	800 m
Rate of fire:	20–30 rounds/min
Penetrative power:	66mm/500m/90°
Manufacturer:	Mauser Werke, Berlin: Rheinmetall, Düsseldorf: Ambi-Budd (chassis), Berlin

Although designated officially as an anti-tank heavy rifle (sPzB), this weapon had all the characteristics of a Pak cannon, i.e. carriage, recoil suppression system and splinter shield. Development began in 1939 at the Mauser Works, Oberndorf; after the first trials with the units in the early summer of 1940 a lightly modified design was introduced in 1941, the "Schwere Panzerbüchse 41". The sPzB 41 fired 2.8-cm shells which passed through a conical barrel to a muzzle of 2-cm diameter, being compressed in the process. In order for this to work, the shell had a soft metal jacket surrounding a hard tungsten-carbide core. The technique increased the muzzle velocity to 1400 m/sec so that 66 mm of steel armour could be penetrated at 500 metres range, but it caused a very high rate of barrel wear and tear. The sPzB 41 was produced with two different chassis. The usual box tail chassis had two large wheels with all-rubber tyres and splinter shield and could be dismantled into five parts

with a few hand movements. The paratroop version had a light metal chassis with small wheels and no shield. Production was halted in 1943 due to the shortage of tungsten after 2997 models had been turned out.

2.8-cm sPzB 41 on spreading-tail chassis.

Sketch of the 2.8-cm sPzB 41 on paratroop chassis

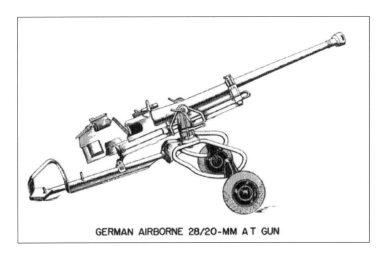

GERMAN AIRBORNE 28/20-MM A T GUN

Southern France, November 1942: sPzB 41 on paratroop chassis in position overlooking a port.

2.5-cm Panzerabwehrkanone 112(f)

Type:	Light Pak
Calibre:	25 mm
Barrel length:	1800 mm (L/72)
Weight:	Firing position: 496 kg
Muzzle velocity:	918 m/sec
Weight of shell:	0.32 kg (PzGr)
Traverse:	60°
Elevation range:	–5°/+21
Effective range:	1800 m
Penetrative power:	40mm/400m/25°
Manufacturer:	Hotchkiss, St Denis.

This Pak was based on a tank gun designed by Hotchkiss towards the end of the First World War but not ready for a series run until 1920. The French Army accepted a modified version in 1934 and introduced it under the designation "Canon léger de 25 antichar SA-L mie 1934". At the outbreak of war the French forces had more than 3000 weapons of the type, and it was also used by the BEF in 1940.

A row of freshly captured 2.5-cm Pak of the Hotchkiss type. Belgium, May 1940. (WKA)

The chassis was so light that it often broke up in the field under motorized tow. Another disadvantage was the poor penetrating power even for 1940. Nevertheless the Wehrmacht took over large numbers as "2.5-cm Pak 112(f)" and used it to arm its occupation troops primarily in France. Numerous very similar "Canon léger de 25 antichar SA-L mie 1937" built by Atelier Puteaux were taken into German service as "2.5-cm Pak 113(f)"; these also had the light chassis. Some Hotchkiss-Pak saw action in North Africa, others were mounted on the light armoured personnel-carriers of the type Sd.Kfz 250.

2.5-cm Pak 112(f) used by German troops in the autumn of 1944 seen at the Museum of War and Resistance, Overloon, Holland.

3.7-cm Panzerabwehrkanone 36

As early as the mid-1920s Rheinmetall had developed a 3.7-cm Pak which came to the Reichwehr in small numbers from 1928. In 1933/34 it was redesigned and turned out in large numbers for the expanding Wehrmacht. The "Pak 36" was a conventional Pak with box tail, all-rubber tyres (first models had wooden wheels) and a 5mm splinter shield. It first saw action in the Spanish civil war in 1937/1938. Large numbers of the weapon went to the Pak-units and by September 1939 it had become the standard Pak of the Wehrmacht.

Because of its small size and light weight it was easy to camouflage and move around while its penetrating power matched that of contemporary guns of the same calibre. In May 1940 the Pak 36 received the nickname "the German Army's door knocker" because of its poor performance against British and French medium and heavy armour. Nevertheless the Pak 36 was operational in large numbers in June 1941 during the attack on the Soviet Union. It was successful against light Russian armour but against better protected types such as the

3.7-cm Pak 36 during pre-war manouevres. Notice the folded back upper part of the splinter shield

T-34, KW-1 and KW-2 practically useless. The penetrative power was increased initially by the introduction of ammunition with a tungsten core (PzGr 40), and from February 1942 the "Stielgranate 41" was used, a large-calibre shell of 8.5 kg stabilized in flight by fins and fired from the muzzle opening. This hollow charge shell (length 738 mm, calibre 159 mm) had 2.3 kg explosive and would go through a maximum of 180 mm steel armour. On account of the muzzle velocity of only 110 m/sec, the enemy tank had to be within 300 metres and approaching.

In March 1942 the production of the Pak 36 was terminated after more than 14,450 examples had

The 3.7-cm Pak was the standard anti-tank gun of the German forces in the first years of the war.

Type:	Light Pak
Calibre:	37 mm
Barrel length:	1665 mm (L/45)
Weight for transport:	440 kg
Weight, firing position:	328 kg
Muzzle velocity:	762 m/sec (PzGr), 1030 m/sec (PzGr 40 tungsten core), 110 m/sec, (StielGr=warhead with shaft 41)
Weight of shell:	0.68 kg (PzGr), 0.354 kg (PzGr 40 with tungsten core), 0.625 kg (AP).
Traverse:	60°
Elevation range:	–8°/+25°
Maximum range:	7000 m
Rate of fire:	20–30 rounds/min
Penetrative power:	48mm/500m/90° (PzGr)
Manufacturer:	Developed by Rheinmetall

been built. Nevertheless the weapon remained in commission until 1945, being employed for its light weight by the paratroop arm and also as a support weapon in Sd.Kfz 250 and 251 half-tracks. Other Pak 36 went to allies of the German Reich amongst them Finland, Rumania and Slovakia. Even before the war Pak 36 had been exported to various countries such as Spain, the Netherlands and the USSR. In the latter the gun was copied under licence and strongly influenced the development of the Red Army's 4.5-cm anti-tank gun. On the Eastern Front captured Soviet 3.7-cm anti-tank guns were designated " 3.7-cm Pak 158(r)", their chassis serving later for infantry guns. In 1937 the USA bought two Pak 36 which served as a basis for the design of the "3.7-cm Pak M3".

Side profile of a 3.7-cm Pak 36 of the Afrika Korps. (WKA)

Stielgranate 41 seen at the National Museum of War and Resistance, Overloon, Holland.

3.7-cm Panzerabwehrkanone 37(t)

Type:	Light Pak
Calibre:	37 mm
Barrel length:	1778 mm (L/47.8)
Weight for transport:	405 kg
Weight, firing position:	370 kg
Muzzle velocity:	750 m/sec (PzGr)
Weight of shell:	0.85 kg (PzGr)
Traverse:	50°
Elevation range:	–8°/+26°
Maximum range:	5000 m
Effective range:	900 m
Rate of fire:	12 rounds/min
Manufacturer:	Skoda Werke, Pilsen

This gun was originally designed by Skoda for the Czech Army and brought into service there in 1937 as "37-mm kanon P.U.V. vz. 37" for non-motorized infantry units, which had to move their anti-tank guns by hand. Typical of Skoda designs was the recoil system above the barrel and the folding spars of the box tail which made the gun more compact for transport. The wooden-spoked wheels gave the weapon an antiquated look, despite that this 3.7-cm Pak was one of the best and most modern guns of its class. After the occupation of Czech territory in March 1939 the Wehrmacht took charge of about 300 cannon of this type and used them under the designation "3.7-cm Pak 37(t)", more came their way in May 1941 in Yugoslavia ("3.7-cm Pak 156(j)". Until April 1940 Skoda turned out another 513 guns for reserve units.

This 3.7-cm Pak(t) without shield was used in the autumn of 1944 by German troops against the advancing Allies near Overloon. Seen at the Nation Museum of War and Resistance, Overloon, Holland.

Obviously brand-new 3.7-cm Pak(t) of a Waffen-SS unit. (WKA)

4.2-cm leichte Panzerabwehrkanone 41

Type:	Light Pak
Calibre:	42/28 mm
Barrel length:	2250 mm (L/55.8)
Weight for transport:	560 kg
Weight, firing position:	560 kg
Muzzle velocity:	1265 m/sec (PzGr)
Weight of shell:	0.336 kg (PzGr)
Traverse:	60°
Elevation range:	-8°/+25°
Maximum range:	7000 m
Effective range:	1000 m
Rate of fire:	10–12 rounds/min
Penetrative power:	87 mm/500 m/90°
Manufacturer:	Billerer & Künz, Aschersleben

The "Pak 41" was the second weapon with a conical barrel introduced by the Wehrmacht. The calibre near the shell chamber was 42 mm and 28 mm at the muzzle. As with the sPzB 41 the so-called "Gerlich principle" provided a higher muzzle velocity and as a result more penetration, although the barrel had to be changed after 1000 rounds. The base was the modified chassis of the 3.7-cm Pak 36, a new double shield with 40 mm spacing between the individual parts being added, raising the resistance to splinters and incoming fire. The weapon was introduced in 1942 and distributed to anti-tank and airborne units.

For parachute drops the later units had special cargo frames which could also be used for the 3.7-cm Pak 36. About two dozen Pak 41 were tested by the Waffen-SS. The main reason for the halting of

production in May 1942 was the lack of tungsten, without which the special hard-core ammunition of the Pak 41 could not be manufactured. Until that point 317 models had been completed from November 1941.

Rear view of the 4.2-cm light Pak 41.

The 4.2-cm Pak based on the 3.7-cm Pak chassis.

4.7-cm Panzerabwehrkanone 35/36 (ö)

Type:	Light Pak
Calibre:	47 mm
Barrel length:	1525 mm (L/32)
Weight for transport:	315 kg
Weight, firing position:	277 kg
Muzzle velocity:	630 m/sec (PzGr), 250 m/sec (HE and hollow charge shells)
Weight of shell:	1.44 kg (PzGr), 2.73 kg (HE and hollow charge)
Traverse:	62°
Elevation range:	–15°/+56°
Maximum range:	700 m
Effective range:	1000 m
Rate of fire:	10 rounds/min
Penetrative power:	43 mm/500 m/90°

This weapon was developed in 1935 by Böhler as a multi-purpose cannon (Pak, infantry- and mountain-gun). Very striking was the (originally) missing splinter shield and the possibility of dismantling the gun into several parts. The wheels could be removed in order to make a more stable firing platform. Before the annexation of Austria the cannon was exported to numerous countries, amongst others Italy (also built there under licence), Rumania, Finland, the Baltic States and the Netherlands. In 1938 the Wehrmacht seized about 300 of these guns in Austria and commissioned them as "4.7-cm Pak 35/36(ö)". Up to when production was halted in

September 1940 Böhler had made another 150. Additional Böhler Pak-guns were captured in the Netherlands in May 1940 ("4.7-cm Pak 187(h)").

4.7-cm Panzerabwehrkanone 36(t)

Although outwardly antiquated, the 4.7-cm Pak 36(t) was one of the world's best anti-tank guns. (Vincent Bourguignon)

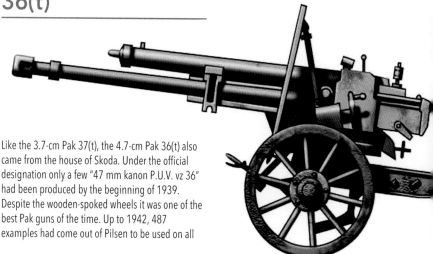

Like the 3.7-cm Pak 37(t), the 4.7-cm Pak 36(t) also came from the house of Skoda. Under the official designation only a few "47 mm kanon P.U.V. vz 36" had been produced by the beginning of 1939. Despite the wooden-spoked wheels it was one of the best Pak guns of the time. Up to 1942, 487 examples had come out of Pilsen to be used on all

A large number of these Wehrmacht Paks were apparently sold to Italy and other Axis allies at the beginning of 1941. When the time came in September 1943 a large number of Italian Böhler Paks (known there as "Cannone 47/32 M35") returned to the Wehrmacht to be known now as "4.7-cm Pak 177(i)": despite hollow charge ammunition having been developed for the gun in Italy it was already obsolescent by then as a Pak gun.

4.7-cm Böhler Pak displayed at Camp Borden, Canada. (Laszlo Nyary)

fronts. Later batches had pneumatic tyres for motorized traction. The Wehrmacht also commissioned captured guns from Yugoslav stocks ("4.7-cm Pak 179(j)"). A speciality of this design was the barrel capable of being traversed 180° to face to the rear over the chassis tail for transport, additionally the outer parts of the chassis tail could be joined together. The Wehrmacht used this Pak (which with its HE shells could also be used as an effective infantry-gun) to arm two self-propelled chassis, the "Panzerjäger 1" on the base of the PzKpfw.1, and a vehicle on the base of a captured Renault R-35 chassis.

Type:	Light Pak
Calibre:	47 mm
Barrel length:	2040 mm (L/43.8)
Weight for transport:	605 kg
Weight, firing position:	590 kg
Muzzle velocity:	775 m/sec (PzGr)
Weight of shell:	1.64 kg (PzGr)
Traverse:	50°
Elevation range:	–8°/+26°
Maximum range:	4000 m
Effective range:	1200 m
Rate of fire:	Not available
Penetrative power:	60 mm/1200 m/90°
Manufacturer:	Skoda Works, Pilsen

5-cm Panzerabwehrkanone 38

Type:	Pak
Calibre:	50 mm
Barrel length:	3000 mm (L/60)
Weight for transport:	1062 kg
Weight, firing position:	986 kg
Muzzle velocity:	835 m/sec (PzGr 39), 1180 m/sec (PzGr 40 tungsten core), 550 m/sec (HE), 160 m/sec (StielGr 42)
Weight of shell:	2.06 kg (PzGr 39), 0.925 kg (PzGr 40, 1.96 kg (HE)
Traverse:	65°
Elevation range:	−8°/+27°
Maximum range:	9400 m
Effective range:	1500 m
Rate of fire:	12–15 rounds/min
Penetrative power:	78 mm/500 m/90° (PzGr 39), 120 mm/ 500 m/90°
Manufacturer:	Developed by Rheinmetall, Düsseldorf

In 1935 Rheinmetall began work on a 5-cm calibre successor to the 3.7-cm Pak. A model designated "Pak 37" (L/45.6) was rejected by the Army Weapons Department and replaced by a new gun with longer barrel (L/60), greater muzzle velocity and a muzzle brake. It was ready for series production in 1939 but did not reach the front before the end of the campaign in the West in the summer of 1940. Initially the "Pak 38" went to the "heavy platoons" of the anti-tank companies.

Built on a conventional box tail chassis with all-rubber tyres, and provided with a third, small tail wheel for manouvring by the crew, the two splinter shield sides were made of 4 mm armour plating with

Front aspect of a 5-cm Pak 38 taken on 17 September 1942, location unknown. (Holger Erdmann collection)

a 25 mm spacing between them. This arrangement increased the protection in comparison to an 8 mm quite substantially. With tungsten hard-core shells (PzGr 40) the Pak 38 was a very effective weapon. The scarcity of tungsten proved a major disadvantage, from 1943 the ammunition was no longer available. Normal AP ammunition (PzGr 39) was adequate against most armour of the Western Allies until 1945, but not against the Soviet T-34 or KW-1. For assaults on heavily armoured targets the hollow-charge grenade fired from the muzzle was specially developed and introduced in March 1943. This "Stielgranate 42" weighed 13.5 kg and had a 2.3 kg hollow charge able to go through 180 mm

armoured steel plate. The very heavy Pak 38 was usually towed by a 1-tonne tractor or occasionally fitted onto it directly, creating a provisional but powerful Pak self-propelled chassis.

Rheinmetall developed the Pak 38 into the tank gun "KwK 39"and, with automatic ammunition supply, into the aircraft cannon "BK 5". Based on the BK-5, Mauser then developed another aircraft cannon, the MK 214 A, which mutated into a flak gun in the final days of the war, but it was never produced in series. As an emergency solution 50 machine-cannons were operational placed on the Gerät 58 chassis. Over 9,500 Pak 38 came to the troops.

5-cm Pak 38 of unknown Afrika Korps unit. (WKA)

A 5-cm Pak 38 deployed in the autumn of 1944 during the fighting in the Netherlands. Nation Museum of War and Resistance, Overloon, Holland.

7.5-cm Panzerabwehrkanone 40

Long before the front troops received the Pak 38, Wehrmacht Command had asked for a more effective weapon, and to Rheinmetall went the contract in 1939 to develop it. For more haste, the Düsseldorf factories built an enlarged version of the Pak 38 with box tail chassis, double splinter shield, large wheels with all-rubber tyres and a low profile. Outwardly the two gun types looked very much alike, the principal differences being the larger muzzle brake, the double splinter shield angled to simplify production and the barrel of the "7.5-cm Pak 40" clamped to the gun cradle. Whereas for the Pak 38 chassis much use had been made of light metals, as a result of their scarcity only steel had been used for the Pak 40. For that reason the Pak 40 was considerably heavier than its forerunner. It required a great effort for the gun crew to shift the Pak 40, therefore recourse was had if possible to a towing vehicle for changes of firing position. During the retreat on the Eastern Front many guns were lost because of sinking into deep mud from where they could not be towed free. As a consequence various self-propelled chassis were made for the Pak 40, for example the vehicles of the "Marder" series. Analogous to the Pak 38, on the basis of the Pak 40 Rheinmetall built a tank gun, the "KwK 40" and "StuK 40", with which for example the versions F2 to J of the PzKpfw.IV, the StuG IV and StuG III from version F/8 were armed. Small numbers of modified Pak 40 were operational as aircraft cannon, for example as armament for the Henschel Hs 129 fighter-bomber.

At the front the Pak 40 was used additionally as a light field-gun ("Feldkanone 40") but was not ideal for the role because of the poor maximum barrel elevation of 22°. In 1944/1945 two field guns were developed based on the Pak 40. The "7.5-cm Feldkanone 7M59" was in its final form a Pak 40 with increased barrel elevation, while the "7.5-cm Feldkanone 7M85" had the barrel of the Pak 40

7.5-cm Pak 40, exhibited at Seneca Falls, New York/USA. (Seth Gaines)

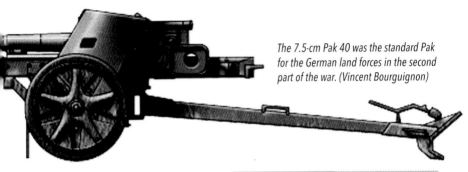

The 7.5-cm Pak 40 was the standard Pak for the German land forces in the second part of the war. (Vincent Bourguignon)

inlaid into the chassis of the 10.5-cm leFH 18/40, which represented a modification of the original Pak 40 chassis. Both these field guns were produced only in very small numbers.

The Pak 40 itself was introduced at the front at the the end of 1941 and from 1943 was the standard Pak gun of the Wehrmacht. It proved itself on all fronts and needed no ammunition with tungsten hard-core (PzGr 40) in order to stop most Allied tanks. Only the heavy Soviet JS-series and late variants of the British "Churchill" presented problems when oncoming frontally. From the beginning of 1942 until May 1945 over 23,300 examples of the long-barrel version of the Pak 40 were turned out, added to which was an unknown quantity of guns for use on self-propelled chassis.

Pak 40 were also operational with Axis allies of the Reich and remnant stocks were to be found long after 1945 in the arsenals of such countries as Albania, Yugoslavia, Rumania, Hungary, Norway, Finland and Czechoslovakia. In the course of Soviet aid in armaments, a number of 7.5-cm Pak 40 even turned up in North Vietnam.

Type:	Heavy Pak
Calibre:	75 mm
Barrel length:	3700 mm (L/46)
Weight for transport:	1500 kg
Weight, firing position:	1425 kg
Muzzle velocity:	750 m/sec (PzGr 39), 930 m/sec (PzGr 40 tungsten core), 550 m/sec (HE)
Weight of shell:	6.8 kg (PzGr 39), 4.1 kg (PzGr 40), 5.74 kg (HE)
Traverse:	65°
Elevation range:	-5°/+22°
Maximum range:	7700 m
Effective range:	2000 m
Rate of fire:	12-15 rounds/min
Penetrative power:	135 mm/500 m/90° (PzGr 39), 154 mm/500 m/90° (PzGr 40)
Manufacturer:	Developed by Rheinmetall, Düsseldorf

7.5-cm Pak 40 protecting a field path. (WKA)

7.5-cm Pak 40 in an Italian location, 1943. (BA)

Eight 7.5-cm Pak 40 captured by the US Army, Igny sur Mer, France, summer 1944. (NARA)

7.5-cm Panzerabwehrkanone 41

The "7.5-cm Pak 41" appeared in 1939 as Krupp's competitor to the Rheinmetall Pak 40. As with the sPzB 41 and the lePak 41, the Krupp gun worked on the Gerlich principle with a conical barrel. The calibre was 75 mm from the breech for a length of 2.95 m, at which point the calibre contracted for the short stretch to 55 mm at the muzzle. The advantage therein was that the typically high wear and tear on the barrel using the Gerlich principle occurred principally in this outer part of the barrel, which was screwed into the rest of it allowing a rapid refit in the field. The Pak 41 was an uncommonly satisfactory weapon whose penetrative power greatly exceeded that of the Pak 40. As with all Paks with a conical barrel, however, a special munition with a tungsten core was required (PzGr 41HK). This metal was practically impossible to obtain by 1942 so that by the end of 1941 only 150

Paks of this type had been turned out. The performance of the Pak 41 with steel-core ammunition (PzGr 41W) was less impressive. After the barrels of the 150 existing specimens were past their best they were either scrapped or the carriages were fitted with Pak 40 barrels.

Type:	Heavy Pak
Calibre:	75 mm
Barrel length:	4322 mm (L/57.6)
Weight, firing position:	1390 kg
Muzzle velocity:	1220 m/sec (PzGr 41 HK), 1230 m/sec (PzGr 41W), 900 m/sec (HE)
Weight of shell:	2.6 kg (PzGr 41 HK), 2.5 kg (PzGr 41 W), 2.65 kg (HE)
Traverse:	60°
Elevation range:	–10°/+18°
Effective range:	2000 m
Rate of fire:	12–14 rounds/min
Penetrative power:	209 mm/500 m/90° or 124 mm/2000 m/90° (PzGr 41 HK)
Manufacturer:	Krupp, Essen

Side profile of the 7.5-cm Pak 41 with conical barrel. (US Army)

The 7.5-cm Pak 41 was a thoroughly efficient gun. The shortage of tungsten prevented it being built in large numbers. (IWM)

7.5-cm Panzerabwehrkanone 97/38

Type:	Heavy Pak
Calibre:	75 mm
Barrel length:	2720 mm (L/36.2
Weight for transoport:	1270 kg
Weight, firing position:	1190 kg
Muzzle velocity:	570 m/sec (PzGr), 450 m/sec (hollow charge shell), 6.19 kg (HE)
Weight of shell:	6.8 kg (PzGr), 4.57 kg (hollow charge shell), 6.19 kg (HE)
Traverse:	60°
Elevation range:	-8°/+25°
Maximum range:	11,000 m
Effective range:	1900 m
Rate of fire:	10-14 rounds/min
Penetrative power:	58 mm/1000 m/60° (PzGr), 90 mm all distances/90° (hollow charge shell).
Original manufacturer:	French national arsenal

As a response to the Soviet T-34 and the KW tanks, in the autumn of 1941 the Army Weapons Department looked for a temporary solution to bridge the gap before the Pak 40 became available. In Poland and France the Wehrmacht had captured thousands of "Canon de 75 mle 1897" which were either put into reserve or commissioned as "7.5-cm FK 97(p), 97(f) or 231 (f)." As their old-fashioned box-tail chassis was not suitable for Pak work or motorized haulage, the barrel was inset into the chassis of the Pak 38. Although a Vielloch muzzle brake was installed to reduce the recoil, the "Pak 97/38" proved highly unstable. The ammunition came from captured stocks, but the Polish shells failed to reach the hoped-for effective speed due to the low muzzle velocity. Therefore a German hollow-charge shell was used which (independent of the range) would go through 90 mm of armour. Nevertheless the Pak 97/38, the first of which came to the front in the summer of 1942, was not popular there and they were passed to units in the rear as soon as the Pak 40 became available in numbers. Smaller quantities

A 7.5-cm Pak captured by the US Army. (US Army)

were also operational in Finland, Hungary, Italy and Rumania. The statistics on the production of the Pak 97/38 are contradictory, and in the literature vary from 700 to 800 examples to as high as 2591. What is confirmed meanwhile is 160 "Pak 97/40" which came into being in 1943 by using the chassis of the Pak 40.

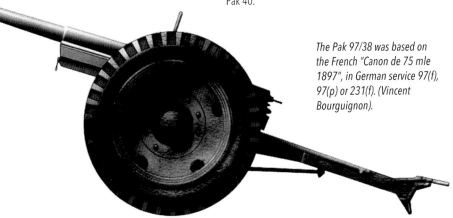

The Pak 97/38 was based on the French "Canon de 75 mle 1897", in German service 97(f), 97(p) or 231(f). (Vincent Bourguignon).

Rear view of a 7.5-cm Pak 97/38 near Lake Ilmen, northern sector of the Eastern Front. In the background is a T-34/76. (WKA)

7.5-cm Panzerabwehrkanone 50

Type:	Heavy Pak
Calibre:	75 mm
Barrel length:	2245 mm (L/30)
Weight for transport:	1095 kg
Weight, firing position:	1095 kg
Muzzle velocity:	450 m/sec
Traverse:	65°
Elevation range:	–8°/+27°
Effective range:	1000 m
Rate of fire:	12–15 rounds/min
Penetrative power:	75 mm/1000 m/90° (hollow charge shell)
Manufacturer:	Developed by Rheinmetall, Düsseldorf

The principal disadvantage of the Pak 40 was its great weight, which made it almost impossible for the gun crew to move it. At the end of 1944 therefore a lighter Pak with a calibre of 7.5 cm surfaced in the Pak units of the infantry. This gun designated "Pak 50" had the Pak 38 5-cm barrel shortened to 2246 mm (L/30) and bored down to 7.5-cm calibre. So that the carriage of the Pak 38 could handle the recoil of a 7.5-cm shell, the barrel was given a muzzle brake. There were two versions of this brake, one with three and the other with five gas deflection surfaces.
The Pak 50 was a typical emergency back-up for the last months of the war. At 1095 kg it was easier to move than the Pak 40, but its penetrative power was unsatisfactory and therefore fulfilled its role only to a very limited extent, for it required hollow charge shells in order to engage enemy tanks. Few models of the Pak 50 were built and they were used mainly as an infantry gun, less as a Pak.

Side profile of the Pak 50. (US Army)

The Pak 50 was fitted with two different muzzle brakes, one with three chambers (above), the other with five. (US Army)

7.62-cm Panzer-abwehrkanone 36(r)

After the beginning of the campaign in the East, German forces captured a large quantity of Soviet "7.62-cm Feldgeschütze 1936" (F-22) which were thrust into service unmodified as "7.62-cm Feldkanone 296(r)" and fired captured ammunition. Because of the lack of a German heavy Pak the Army Weapons Department decided at the end of 1941 that German industry should convert the weapon for anti-tank work. The guns were then given a larger breech for new ammunition manufactured in Germany with higher muzzle velocity. In order to limit the greater recoil, the cradle was reinforced and most guns given a muzzle brake. The wheels for

Type:	Heavy Pak
Barrel length:	76.2 mm
Barrel length:	3895 mm (L/51)
Weight, firing position:	1710 kg
Muzzle velocity:	740 m/sec (PzGr 39 7, 62 cm), 930 m/sec (PzGr 40, 7.62 cm) 550 m/sec (HE)
Weight of shell:	7.54 kg (PzGr 39, 7.62 cm), 4.15 kg (PzGr 40 7.62 cm), 6.2 kg (HE)
Traverse:	60°
Elevation range:	–6°/+18°
Maximum range:	10,400 m
Effective range:	2500 m
Rate of fire:	10–12 rounds/min
Penetrative power:	120 mm/500 m/90°, 78 mm/2500 m/90° (both PzGr 39, 7.62 cm).
Original manufacturer:	Soviet State firms

elevation and traversing were transferred to the left side where the aiming devices were located so that a single man could handle them. In addition the splinter shield was changed and the elevation of the barrel limited to +18°. The first modified guns of the type were delivered in the spring of 1942 and did all that was hoped of them.

Up to 1944 a total of 560 captured field guns were converted into "Pak 36(r)" while another 800 were used as armament for various anti-tank self-propelled chassis. The planned production of replicas in the Reich never came about, although another 300 or so captured Soviet "7.62-cm Feldkanonen 297(r)" were converted and known as "Pak 39(r)".

Front and rear view of a 7.62 cm Pak 36(r). (Holger Erdmann collection)

8-cm Panzerabwehrwerfer 600

Type:	Heavy Pak
Calibre:	81.4 cm
Barrel length:	2950 mm (L/36.2)
Weight for transport:	640 kg
Weight, firing position:	630 kg
Muzzle velocity:	520 m/sec (hollow charge)
	420 m/sec (HE)
Weight of shell:	2.7 kg (hollow charge),
	4.46 kg (HE)
Traverse:	55°
Elevation range:	-6°/+32°
Maximum range:	6000 m
Effective range:	800 m
Rate of fire:	6-8 rounds/min
Penetrative power:	145 mm/all distances/90°
	(hollow charge)
Manufacturer:	Rheinmetall, Düsseldorf:
	R.Wolf, Magdeburg.

The "PAW 600" (also "Panzerabwehrwurfkanone 8H63") came about because the conventional Pak, though becoming more effective as the war went on, was also heavier and more unwieldy. On the other hand light guns betrayed their location by the expelled propellant gases and required too much powder. In 1943 the designers at Rheinmetall came up with the High-Low Pressure System which combined the shell casing over a perforated steel plate with a hollow charged shell stabilized by fins. When the charge in the shell casing was ignited, the perforated steel plate ensured that the pressure in the barrel was substantially less than the pressure in the rear chamber. This allowed the barrel (and with it the carriage) to be of lighter construction. Fin-stabilized shells also permitted the use of a smooth bore barrel which could be manufactured quicker and less problematically. Although the range in comparison to conventional Pak was much less, at the end of 1944 the Army Weapons Department decided to make the PAW 600 into the standard Pak. By the end of the war only 260 of these weapons had been turned out, of which probably only just over a hundred reached the front. Difficulties at the factories caused by war circumstances led to problems with the ammunition holding its course when fired ("Treffsicherheit"). In 1945 Krupp developed the "10-cm PWK 10H 64" which worked on a similar principle, made never made it to series production.

Some barrels of the PAw 600 wdre fitted on the chassis of the 5-cm Pak 38 and were then given the muzzle brake of the 7.5-cm Pak 40

8.8-cm Panzerabwehrkanone 43

The "Pak 43" had its origins as a flak gun ("Gerät 42") developed by Krupp in 1940 and which had been designed as a competitor to Rheinmetall's later "Flak 41". Because of changes in the specification, Krupp removed the design from the competition and realized plans to finish the gun as a flak in modified form also capable of being deployed as a Pak or a vehicular KwK. The Army Weapons Department accepted the Pak design at the beginning of 1943.

Now known as the "Pak 43", it had a barrel 6.61 (L/71) metres in length with a muzzle velocity of 1000 m/sec using the PzGr 39/43 shell. When the lighter PzGr 40/43 was fired, which had a tungsten core (and was therefore not often used), the muzzle velocity was 1130 m/sec. The Pak 43 rested on a cross-chassis loaded on two single-axis limbers, from where it could also fire if circumstances dictated. Although the cross-chassis was very expensive to

manufacture, it gave the Pak 43 a very low profile of only 1.7 metres and allowed a 360° traverse. The towed Pak 43 was first used at the front in mid-1943 although in February 1943 it had been lightly modified for use on an anti-tank self-propelled chassis known as "Hornisse" (hornet) or "Nashorn" (rhino).

As the manufacture of the cross-chassis could not meet the demand, at the end of 1943 the "Pak 43/41" was introduced as an addition. This had some changes at the breech, a modified spreading tail chassis from the 10.5-cm leFH 18, and wheels from the 15-cm sFH 18. This improvised chassis gave the Pak an overall increase in height of only 28 cms, but now it looked so big that the troops gave it the nickname "barn door". Ballistically both versions were identical and proved so uncommonly powerful in action that many experts identified the Pak 43 as the best Pak gun of the Second World War. Even at long range it could destroy the best protected enemy tank. In combat with medium tanks such as the T-34 it has been reported that a direct hit tore off the turret from the bodywork. There are also reports that T-34's were destroyed at a range of 3500 metres. The other side of the coin was the great weight, both versions of the Pak 43 being so heavy that they could

An 8.8-cm Pak 43/1 captured by US troops on Omaha Beach, June 1944. (NARA)

This photograph of an 8.8-cm Pak 43/1 comes from an old US Army handbook. (US Army)

only be moved by half-track tractors. Only lightly modified, the Pak 43 was used in panzers of the type "Ferdinand" and "Jagdpanther". In a modified form they were the main weapon of the "Tiger II". By the war's end a total of 2098 Pak 43 and 1403 Pak 43/41 had been turned out.

Top and also page 71, same caption) 8.8-cm Pak 43 exhibited at the Aberdeen Proving Ground, Maryland, USA. (Seth Gaines)

Type:	Heavy Pak
Calibre:	88 mm
Barrel length:	6610 mm (L/71)
Weight for transport:	4750 kg (Pak 43)
Weight, firing position:	3650 kg (Pak 43) 4380 kg (Pak 43/41)
Muzzle velocity:	1000 m/sec (PzGr 39/43); 1130 m/sec (PzGr 40/43); 750 m/sec (HE 43)
Weight of shell:	10.16 kg (PzGr 39/43), 7.3 kg (PzGr 40/43), 9.4 kg (HE 43)
Traverse:	360° (Pak 43), 56° (Pak 43/41)
Elevation range:	–8°/+40° (Pak 43), –5°/+38 (Pak 43/41)
Maximum range:	15,300 m
Effective range:	2500 m
Rate of fire:	6–10 rounds/min
Pentrative power:	190 mm/1000 m/90° (PzGr 39/43), 241 mm/ 1000 m/90° (PzGr 40/43).
Manufacturer:	Krupp, Essen; Henschel, Kassel; Weserhüte, Bad Oeynhausen; Rheinmetall, Düsseldorf.

8.8-cm Pak 43/1 auf dem Aberdeen Proving Ground, Maryland/USA. (Seth Gaines)

12.8-cm Panzerabwehrkanone 80

80" was a design masterpiece and belongs amongst the most powerful Pak ever developed. Although its penetrative power was not much superior to that of the Pak 43, at long ranges the 12.8-cm PzGr 43 shell, three times heavier than the shell fired by the Pak

In 1943 the Army Weapons Department issued contracts to Krupp and Rheinmetall for a field cannon superior to the Red Army's 12.2-cm guns Type A-19. Following the appearance of new Soviet tanks, the thrust of the development turned increasingly towards a Pak. At the end of 1944 both concerns presented very similar prototypes, each with cross-chassis for a 360° traverse. The Krupp design had four wheels, the Rheinmetall chassis six. After the intitial testing the choice for further development and pre-series production fell on the Krupp gun, but in the course of these trials it became obvious that a long-barrelled Pak over ten tonnes in weight was not a reasonable proposition under field conditions. Therefore although a few guns were manufactured, they were not run off in series. All the same, the "Pak

Type:	Heavy Pak
Calibre:	128 mm
Barrel length:	7023 mm (L/55)
Weight for transport:	10,160 kg
Weight, firing posiiton:	10,160 kg
Muzzle velocity:	920 m/sec (PzGr 43), 750 m/sec (HE)
Weight of shell:	28.3 kg (PzGr 43), 28 kg (HE)
Traverse:	360°
Elevation range:	-7.5°/+45°
Maximum range:	24,410 m
Rate of fire:	5 rounds/min
Penetrative power:	202 mm/1000 m/90°, 187 mm/1500 m/90° (PzGr 43)
Manufacturer:	Krupp, Breslau Works

43, had a far greater impact on the target. Alongside "Pak 80", this weapon was also known as "12.8-cm Pak 43", "Pak 44" "Kanone 44" or "Panzerjägerkanone 44".

One of the 12.8-cm Pak 80 (Krupp version) captured by the US Army; above, ready to transport , below, in firing position. (NARA)

7.5-cm Feldkanone 16 n.A.

Type:	Light field gun
Calibre:	75 mm
Barrel length:	2700 mm (L/36)
Weight for transport:	2415 kg
Weight, firing position:	662 m/sec
Muzzle velocity:	662 m/sec
Weight of shell:	5.83 kg (HE)
Traverse:	4°
Elevation range:	–9°/+44°
Maximum range:	12,875 m
Rate of fire:	10–12 rounds/min
Manufacturer:	Rheinmetall, Düsseldorf

The original "Feldkanone 16" (FK 16) was a 7.7-cm calibre veteran of the First World War. In 1919 the remaining guns were taken over by the Reichswehr and not modified. In 1934 Rheinmetall fitted a large number of them with new 7.5-cm barrels, the weapon now being designated "FK 16 neue Art" (n.A.= new type). These guns were intended as horse-drawn artillery so that neither the box-tail carriage needed redesigning nor the wooden spoked wheels to be fitted with tyres for motorized haulage. Specially striking were single seats either side of the barrel ahead of the splinter shield for the gunners. During the war guns of this type were usually employed for training, with rearward units or incorporated into coastal defences such as the Atlantic Wall although a number remained with front troops until 1945. A few FK 16 in their original state were still to be found with the Wehrmacht well into the war. FK 16 which had been given to Belgium as war reparations after the Great War, and which had been fitted with new 7.5-cm calibre barrels by Cockerills during the 1930s, were taken over as "7.5-cm FK 234(b)" after the Belgians surrendered in May 1940.

7.5-cm FK 16 n.A. during manouevres in the Reich. (WKA)

7.5-cm leichte Feldkanone 18

Type:	Light field gun
Calibre:	75 mm
Barrel length:	1940 mm (L/26)
Weight for transport:	2010 kg
Weight, firing position:	1120 kg
Muzzle velocity:	426 m/sec
Weight of shell:	5.83 kg (HE)
Traverse:	60°
Elevation range:	–5°/+45°
Maximum range:	9425 m
Rate of fire:	4–5 rounds/min
Manufacturer:	Krupp, Essen.

By 1930 Krupp had begun work on a successor to the FK 16. There was no great urgency for the development and so the first series batch was not run off until 1938. The "FK 18" had a special chassis in which the axle spring was disarticulated when the tail beams were opened. Because the was intended to be horse-drawn, it was given wooden spoked wheels with steel rims. The FK 18 was significantly lighter than the "FK 16 n.A.", but its maximum range was less. Outwardly it had the characteristic look of German guns of the time, the recoil brake being in the cradle under barrel and the repositioning spring above the barrel. The FK 18 remained in production only until 1940 and was not manufactured in large numbers although even in 1945 there were some still to be found at the front.

Rear view of a 7.5-cm FK 18 from an old Wehrmacht handbook. (WKA)

75 ■

7.5-cm leichte Feldkanone 38

Type:	Light field gun
Calibre:	75 mm
Barrel length:	2550 mm (L/34)
Weight for transport:	1860 kg
Weight, firing position:	1366 kg
Muzzle velocity:	605 m/sec
Weight of shell:	5.83 kg (HE), 4.6 kg (hollow charge)
Traverse:	50°
Elevation range:	−5°/+45°
Maximum range:	11,500 m
Rate of fire:	10-12 rounds/min
Manufacturer:	Krupp, Essen

In 1938 Krupp designed a refined version of the 7.5-cm FK 18 with longer barrel and muzzle brake for the export market. By September 1939 Brazil had received 65 guns of this type. The design had a spreading chassis with riveted box-trail beams. The tail spurs could be folded back over the beams to shorten the length of the carriage for transport. As was common with German guns of the period this export model also had recoil brake and return spring below and above the barrel respectively. Besides wheels with wooden spokes and steel rims for horse haulage, some were given cast steel spokes and all-rubber tyres. Under contract to the Army Weapons department in 1942, Krupp reproduced a fresh batch of around 80 guns designated "7.5-cm Feldkanone 38" by the Wehrmacht. Manufacture was then terminated. In 1945 there were still 26 of these guns on the Wehrmacht books.

FK 38 with closed and open tail-legs with spurs.

7.62-cm Feldkanone 297(r)

Type:	Light field gun
Calibre:	76.2 mm
Barrel length:	3200 mm (L/42)
Weight for transport:	2350 kg
Weight, firing position:	1570 kg
Muzzle velocity:	680 m/sec (HE)
Weight of shell:	6.2 kg (HE)
Traverse:	57°
Elevation range:	-6°/+45°
Maximum range:	13,290 m
Rate of fire: up to	25 rounds/min
Original manufacturer:	Soviet State firms

Together with a large number of Soviet 7.62-cm field guns of the 1936 model (F-22), in the initial phase of the war against the Soviet Union German troops also captured hundreds of 7.62-cm field guns of the rather lighter 1939 successor model (USV). Most of these efficient and modern guns were then employed by the Wehrmacht in their original role as field guns. The Wehrmacht books for March 1944 have 359 guns of this type "7.62-cm FK 297(r)". Often they were equipped with muzzle brakes in German service. Analogous to the 7.62-cm Pak 36(r), around 300 7.62-cm Feldkanone 297(r) were converted to Pak and given the designation "Pak 39(r)". Amongst the modifications were an enlarging of the chamber in order to take the larger German propellant and equipping with the muzzle brake. The elevation and traverse wheels were moved to the left side of the gun where the gunsight was located to enable one-man operation. The penetrative power was no so good as the Pak 36(r) because of the shorter barrel and lesser muzzle velocity.

Caen, Normandy, August 1944. Three members of the Royal Canadian Ordnance Corps, 1 Canadian Army, examine captured weapons of 89. Inf.Div. (General Heinrichs). Left foreground is the chassis tail of a 7.5-cm Pak, in the right foreground a 7.62-cm FK 297(r). In the background are two 12.2-cm sFH 396(r) and in the centre another 7.62-cm FK 297(r). At the rear two 15-cm sFH 13/1 on Gw Lr.S(f) can be made out (Sf.Kfz 135/1). (National Archives of Canada).

7.62-cm Pak 39(r) of a Luftwaffe field division.

8.76-cm Feldkanone 280(e)

Type:	Field gun
Calibre:	87.6 mm
Barrel length:	2716 mm (L/31)
Weight of gun:	1800 kg
Muzzle velocity:	532 m/sec (maximum propellant), 453 m/sec (normal propellant).
Weight of shell:	11.34 kg (HE)
Traverse:	360° (on baseplate for firing) otherwise 8°
Elevation range:	–5°/+45°
Maximum range:	12,250 m (maximum propellant), 10,790 m (normal propellant)
Rate of fire:	12–14 rounds/min
Maunfacturer:	Various British Government arsenals

The British "Ordnance QF 25 pdr" got its name from the approximate weight of shell. It was introduced into the British Army in 1938 and became the standard field gun of the British Empire forces in the Second World War. (NB. Author says "Commonwealth", wasn't this a post-war thing?TR). 12,000 of them had been built by the war's end. The weapon proved itself very successful in action, being robust and reliable and was much favoured by the troops. Additionally the QF 25 was one of the first British guns which could double as a howitzer. Although the box-trail chassis looked antiquated, it allowed a large elevation (enabling the gun to serve as a howitzer) and had a firing platform on the underside so that the whole gun could be quickly traversed the full 360° and used in the anti-tank role, which often happened in the first years of the war. This versatility made the 25-pounders into much sought-after specimens: the Wehrmacht captured a large number of these guns in France, Greece and North Africa, redesignating them "8.76-cm FK 280(e)". Whole artillery regiments were equipped with them: for some time all the artillery of 90.Light Div/Afrika Korps consisted of captured British 25-pounders and Soviet 7.62-cm field guns.

An 8.76-cm FK 280(e) battery with the Afrika Korps (NARA)

10.5-cm leichte Feldhaubitze 16

Type:	Light field howitzer
Calibre:	105 mm
Barrel length:	310 mm (L/22)
Weight for transport:	2300 kg
Weight, firing position:	1525 kg
Muzzle velocity:	395 m/sec
Weight of shell:	14.81 kg (HE)
Traverse:	4°
Elevation range:	-9°/+40°
Maximum range:	9225 m
Rate of fire:	8-10 rounds/min
Manufacturer:	Krupp, Essen

The le FH 16 was another veteran of the Great War which served the Wehrmacht until 1945. Designed and built by Krupp, the 10.5-cm leFH 16 used the almost unchanged box chassis of the 7.5-cm FK 16 for haulage by horses, its wooden-spoked, steel-rimmed wheels not being suitable for motor traction. As with the 75 mm howitzer, the gun had two seats for gunners ahead of the splinter shield. Until superseded by the leFH 18, this gun was the standard field howitzer of the Wehrmacht. After 1940 most leFH 16 were then passed to training units or rearward troops, while many went later to the Atlantic Wall as coastal guns. Field howitzers of this type which had gone to Belgium as reparations after the First World War were modernized there in the 1930s (amongst other things fitted with pneumatic tyres) and then returned to Germany in 1940 as "10.5-cm leFH 327(b)".

A 10.5-cm leFH 16 battery during exercises in the Reich. (WKA)

10.5-cm leichte Feldhaubitze 18, 18M and 18/40

The "leFH 18" and its variants (leFH 18M and leFH 18/40) were the standard field howitzers of the Wehrmacht at divisional level and belonged amongst the most common German guns of the time. Rheinmetall began design work in 1929 but the guns did not reach the Wehrmacht until 1935. The leFH 18 was a conventional design with spreading chassis beams and hydraulic recoil suppression system. Equipped at first with wooden-spoked wheels and steel rims, later versions had cast steel spokes and all-rubber tyres. All leFH 18 types fired ammunition with a choice of propellant. The first wartime experiences brought the demand for longer range, resulting in a new version with muzzle brake design developed in 1940 with 1.77 kg heavier propellant. Additionally the barrel return and recoil suppression systems were reinforced and a new long range shell (FH Gr.Fern) introduced. This enabled an increase in muzzle

10.5-cm leFH 18 being fired. (WKA)

velocity to 540 m/sec which upped the range by 1650 m to 12,325 metres. Besides newly built howitzers a selection of existing guns were fitted with a muzzle brake. In order to raise its effectiveness and make possible the use of lesser-calibre shells, the shape of the muzzle brake was changed several times in the course of production. Besides the range the very heavy weight of the leFH 18 was disadvantageous as was proved in the trackless conditions on the Eastern Front. Therefore in 1943 work on a lighter version was taken in hand using the little changed lower chassis of the 7.5-cm Pak 40. The upper carriage and barrel on the other hand came from the leFH 18M. This variant known as the "leFH 18/40" had advantages in production but its weight was not much lower. Despite an improved muzzle brake the Pak chassis did not meet long term requirements, its durability and steadfastness not being good. The leFH 18 was also built on various artillery self-propelled chassis, the best known of these undoubtedly being the "Wespe".

The captured chassis from about eighty 10.5-cm howitzers which Krupp had exported to the Netherlands were fitted with leFH 18M barrels and designated "10.5-cm leFH 18/39" by the Wehrmacht.

Type:	Light field howitzer
Calibre:	105 mm
Barrel length:	2941 mm (L/28) without, 3308 mm with muzzle brake
Weight for transport:	3490 kg
Weight, firing position:	2065 kg
Muzzle velocity:	470 m/sec (540 m/sec 18M model)
Weight of shell:	14.81 kg (HE)
Traverse:	56°
Elevation range:	–5°/+42°
Maximum range:	10,675 , (12,325 m 18M model)
Rate of fire:	4 to 6 rounds/min
Manufacturer:	Developed by Rheinmetall, Düsseldorf

The "leFH 18/42", based finally on the leFH 18 chassis, was given a new longer L/31 barrel with a large muzzle brake having numerous slits. This design was turned down by the Army Weapons

10.5-cm leFH 18 in the museum at Drzonow, Poland. (PD)

Department, however, whose specifications for a light howitzer had now changed.

By the war's end a total of 11,831 leFH 18 and 18M, and 10,265 leH 18/40 had been produced.

Before 1939 leFH 18 had been exported to Chile, Argentina and Spain. During the Second World War Hungary, Bulgaria and Finland also commissioned the leFH 18. Even after the war, guns of this type were used for years, as for example in Yugoslavia, Czechoslovakia, Chile, Argentina, Austria, Sweden and Portugal.

(top and bottom) 10.5-cm leFH 18M with all-rubber tyres and muzzle brake. (US Army)

Krupp version (where details vary from above):	
Weight for transport:	2300 kg
Weight, firing position:	1900 kg
Muzzle velocity:	540 m/sec
Traverse:	60°
Maximum range:	12,325 m
Manufacturer:	Krupp, Markstädt Works, Schichau, Elbing and elsewhere.

10.5-cm leFH 18/40 in the National Museum of War and Resistance, Overloon, Netherlands.

10.5-cm leichte Haubitze 43

Type:	Light field howitzer
Calibre:	105 mm
Barrel length:	3675 mm (L/35)
Weight of gun:	2300 kg
Muzzle velocity:	610 m/sec
Weight of shell:	14.81 kg (HE)
Traverse:	360°
Elevation range:	–5°/+75°
Maximum range:	13,000 m
Rate of fire:	6.8 rounds/min
Manufacturer:	Skoda Works, Pilsen

In 1942 the Army Weapons Department ordered the development of a successor to the leFH 18. The prototype presented by Rheinmetall ("leFH 42") was substantially lighter and had a somewhat longer range than the leFH 18, but was declined based on experiences on the Eastern Front. At the end of 1943 the Department then ordered that the gun be made traversable through 360° and able to fire in the upper register (+45°). The Pak ability and range were also to be much improved. The Skoda design had a new kind of carriage with four beams, the front two being folded together below the barrel for transport. Return spring and recoil suppression system where located in the cradle below the barrel: in order to avoid the barrel coming into contact with the ground when firing in the upper register, three different recoil lengths could be selected. Krupp presented two different designs. The first was based on the 8.8-cm Pak 43 cross-chassis in which the barrel of the leFH 18/40 was inset, the second had a new carriage (similar to that of the Skoda design) and the barrel of Rheinmetall's leFh 42. Although very modern and pointing in the right direction, none of three models had been completed by the war's end.

Although facing in the right direction in conception, the le FH43 went no further than the prototype stage.

10-cm leichte Haubitze 14/19(t)

Type:	Light field howitzer
Calibre:	100 mm
Barrel length:	2400 mm (L/24)
Weight for transport:	2855 kg
Weight, firing position:	1490 kg
Muzzle velocity:	395 m/sec
Weight of shell:	16 kg (HE)
Traverse:	5°
Elevation range:	-7°/+48°
Maximum range:	9800 m
Rate of fire:	8 rounds/min
Manufacturer:	Skoda Works, Pilsen.

The origin of this weapon was the Skoda "Haubitze M1914" designed before the First World War which continued in use in Austria, Czechoslovakia, Poland, Rumania and Italy after the dissolution of the Habsburg Empire. Some of them were still in service in the Second World War having been captured by the Wehrmacht which labelled them "leFH 14(ö)" (from Austria) or "leFH 315(i)" (from Italy).

Skoda modernized the original 1919 design with a longer barrel, an improved recoil suppression system, longer carriage tail beams and new traversing and elevation gear. These howitzers ("houfnice vz 14/19") were not only introduced into the Czechoslovak Army, but were additionally exported in large numbers to Poland, Yugoslavia and Greece.

After the annexation of Czechoslovakia, 382 howitzers of this type were seized as "leFH 14/19(f)" and used at the front until 1941 together with 676 specimens of "leFH 14/19(p)" captured in Poland. Along with the "leFH 318(g)" and leFH316(j)" types from Greece and Yugoslavia, howitzers of this type then went to reserve or training units or were installed at the Atlantic Wall.

10-cm leFH 14/19 at the War Museum, Athens. (Konstantinos Stampoulis)

10-cm Kanone 17

This Krupp development dates from 1916 and was used by the Wehrmacht until 1945 although after 1940 most were with reserve units or in service as coastal artillery. The "10-cm Kanone 17" used the practically unchanged carriage of its forerunner, the K14, and was dismantled into two parts (barrel and carriage) for horse towage. Because the carriage was expensive to produce, Krupp had designed a simplified version, the "K17/04" introduced in the late summer of 1917. A total of only 182 of both variants had been manufactured by November 1918. According to the conditions of the Treaty of Versailles, Germany had to scrap all guns of this type or sell them, and both Sweden and Rumania obtained some on favourable terms. Most of the K 17 were hidden from the Allies, however, and these

Type:	Heavy field gun
Calibre:	105 mm
Barrel length:	4725 mm (L/45)
Weight, firing position:	3300 kg
Muzzle velocity:	650 m/sec (HE)
Weight of shell:	18.5 kg (HE)
Traverse:	6°
Elevation range:	−2°/+45°
Maximum range:	16,500 m
Rate of fire:	not available
Manufacturer:	Krupp, Essen

eventually found their way to the Reichswehr and then the Wehrmacht. Some of the 10-cm Kanonen 17 also came from Austria, which had received a number of guns of this type during the First World War. After the annexation of Austria in March 1938, these were repossessed by the Wehrmacht.

A 10-cm K 17 in the coastal defence role, northern Norway 1941. (BA)

Two views of a 10-cm Kanone 17 exhibited at Gonzales/Texas. (Seth Gaines).

10-cm schwere Kanone 18

Type:	Heavy field gun
Calibre:	105 mm
Barrel length:	5460 mm (L/52)
Weight for transport:	6434 kg
Weight, firing position:	5642 kg
Muzzle velocity:	835 m/sec (HE)
Weight of shell:	15.14 kg (HE), 15.56 (AP)
Traverse:	60°
Elevation range:	0°/+45°
Maximum range:	19,075 m
Rate of fire:	6 rounds/min
Manufacturers:	Developed by Rheinmetall, Düsseldorf and Krupp, Essen. Mainly turned out by the Spreewerke, Berlin.

In 1926 the Reichswehr ordered from Krupp and Rheinmetall a new 10-cm cannon eventually introduced in 1933. Interestingly neither of the two designs won through, but finally the Reichswehr opted for the compromise of the Krupp spreading chassis with a Rheinmetall barrel, the carriage also finding use for the 15-cm sFH 18. As with other guns, there were two kinds of wheels depending on the means of transport. For horse-drawn artillery the "sK 18" was separated into two parts, for motor traction the barrel was retracted for better weight distribution. The maximum range of the sK 19 was measured at over 19 kilometres, but not the performance of the approximately 15 kg shell at the target. Production was terminated in 1943: at the outbreak of war the troops had 702 units. Until production was halted, according to the source consulted either 732 or 1433 more were built. Another version with even longer range, 21 kilometres, was the "sK 18/40" (later "sK 42") turned out in small numbers from 1941. After 1945 Bulgaria and Albania commissioned some sK 18.

10-cm K 18 with all-rubber tyres for motor traction in a barracks.(WKA)

Front view of the 10-cm K 18 with iron rims.

10-cm K18 during shooting training at a barracks, 1936.

89 ◼◼

10-cm schwere Kanone 35(t)

This Skoda design was commissioned by the Czech armed forces as "10.5-cm hruby kanon vz. 35" in the mid-1930s. At this time the Yugoslavs also obtained a number. It was a very modern design with spreading chassis and intended only for motor towage. It is therefore no surprise that after the invasion of Czechoslovakia in March 1939 the Wehrmacht seized all available examples of the gun and put it into commission as "10.5-cm sK 35(t)". 36 of them went to the new Slovakian Army. Skoda continued the production of the model under German supervision until 1941 and delivered an

A 10.5-cm sK 35(t) in a concrete emplacement on the Atlantic Wall, Northern France, August 1941. (BA)

unknown quantity of these guns to the Wehrmacht. Up until the end of the Balkans campaign in May 1941 the gun was frequently to be found with front units though afterwards increasingly for coastal defence, e.g. at the Atlantic Wall, or for training. Weapons of this type captured in Yugoslavia and out into German service were designated "10.5-cm K 339(j)".

Type:	Heavy field gun
Calibre:	105 mm
Barrel length:	4400 mm (L/42)
Weight, firing position:	4200 kg
Muzzle velocity:	730 m/sec (HE)
Weight of shell:	18 kg (HE)
Traverse:	50°
Elevation range:	–6°/+42°
Maximum range:	18,100 m
Rate of fire:	8 rounds/min
Manufacturer:	Skoda, Pilsen.

Skoda continued to turn out the 10.5-cm sK 35(t) for the Wehrmacht until 1941.

12.8-cm Kanone 81/1 and 81/2

Type:	Heavy field gun
Calibre:	128 mm
Barrel length:	7023 mm (L/55)
Weight, firing position:	8300 kg
Muzzle velocity:	920 m/sec (PzGr 43-AP)
	750 m/sec (HE)
Weight of shell:	28.3 kg (AP) 28 kg (HE)
Traverse:	40°
Elevation range:	-4°/+45°
Maximum range:	about 24 kms (HE)
Rate of fire:	5 rounds/min
Manufacturer:	unknown

The Kanone 81 was based on the variants of the "12.8-cm Pak 80" or "Pak 44" (q.v.) planned for use on heavy fighting vehicles such as the "Jagdtiger" or "Maus". Shortly before the end of the war, weapons of this kind were put on the chassis of two different captured guns in order to achieve an efficient combination of field gun and Pak. The variant

"K81/1" was based on the carriage for the French "Canon de 155 GPF-T", designated "15.5-cm K 418(f)" by the Wehrmacht, the other used the chassis of Soviet 15.2-cm howitzers of the type "ML-20", designated "KH 433(r)" by the Wehrmacht. Both versions were only a provisional measure but enormously powerful for their outstanding ballistic performance. The number of 12.8-cm 81/1 and 81/2 guns built in the last months of the war cannot be ascertained but would probably not have been much more than a dozen.

12.8-cm K 81/2 guns captured by the US Army in the last days of the war. (NARA)

15-cm schwere Haubitze 13

Type:	Heavy field howitzer
Calibre:	149.7 mm
Barrel length:	2550 mm (L/17)
Weight, firing position:	2270 kg
Muzzle velocity:	390 m/sec
Weight of shell:	39.17 kg (HE)
Traverse:	7°
Elevation range:	0°/+45°
Maximum range:	8900 m
Rate of fire:	3 rounds/min
Manufacturer:	Krupp, Essen

The first guns of this type were already with the German Army by 1914, but from 1917 an improved version with longer barrel was built, this seeing service with the Reichswehr after the war. The "sFH 13" was conceived as horse-drawn and therefore relatively light for its calibre. In order to achieve this, the Krupp designers had to accept a reduction in the maximum range. The sFH 13, although successful, was obsolete by the outbreak of the Second World War and the weapons were generally to be found in coastal defence units although individual guns served at the front for years. Howitzers of this type were also used as armament on artillery self-propelled chassis such as the "15-cm sFH 13 auf Geschützwagen Lorraine". The sFH 13 captured in Belgium and Holland were commissioned into German service as "sFH409(b) and sFH406h)".

15-cm sFH 13 exhibited at Emporia/Virginia, USA (Seth Gaines)

15-cm schwere Feldhaubitze 18

The "sFH 18" entered service with the Wehrmacht in 1935 and was based on a synthesis of two competing designs by Rheinmetall and Krupp from the 1920s. Neither had completely convinced the Army Weapons Department and so it was decided to combine the best elements of each, as a result of which the gun had a Krupp carriage and a Rheinmetall barrel. The " sFH 18" was a solid, conservative design with spreading tail and all-rubber tyres , the chassis being unsuitable for fast towing due to the absence of axle suspension while the weight at 5500 kg was too heavy to be horse-drawn. Nevertheless the "sFH 18" and the "leFH 18" became the standard guns of the Wehrmacht divisional artillery. For a gun of this type the maximum range of 13,250 metres was too short, as become painfully obvious in the fighting on the Eastern Front. Comparable Red Army guns such as the 15.2-cm howitzer "ML-20" or the 12.2-cm Kanone "A-19" had a much longer reach. From 1942 attempts were made to design a more effective

Type:	Heavy field howitzer
Calibre:	149 mm
Barrel length:	4400 mm (L/29.5)
Weight for transport:	6304 kg
Weight, firing position:	5512 kg
Muzzle velocity:	520 m/sec
Weight of shell:	43.5 kg (HE), 24.63 kg (HL=hollow charge), 38.97 kg (NbGr=smoke shell)
Traverse:	60°
Elevation range:	–3°/+45°
Maximum range:	13,326 m
Rate of fire:	4 rounds/min
Manufacturer:	Developed by Krupp, Essen (carriage) and Rheinmetall, Düsseldorf (barrel). Completed by Spreewerke, Berlin; MAN, Augsburg; Skoda-Werke, Dubnica; Dörries-Fullner, Bad Warmbrunn.

successor (e.g. "sFH 43" and "sFH 44") but these went no further than the model stage. Other attempts aimed at lengthening the range. For this purpose the weapon received a muzzle brake ("sFH

A 15-cm SFH 18 battery on artillery exercises in the Reich. (WKA)

18M") and a changeable sheath for the chamber so that more propellant could be used to up the range to 15,100 metres. Despite the muzzle brake the recoil suppression system proved inadequate in the long run to hold the increased recoil force, resulting in serious damage to the carriage. Additionally for the first time ammunition with rocket propellant was introduced globally for the "sFH 18" (15-cm RGr 19, weight 45.25 kg) which while increasing the range lacked accuracy and was heavy on wear and tear. Although the howitzer no longer met the requirements, the Wehrmacht lacked an alternative and so continued using it to the end. When the war broke out the forces had 1353 "sFH 18" and by May 1945 the number now totalled more than 5400 howitzers. From 1943 additionally over 1200 lightly modified "sFH 18/1" were produced for fitting in the self-propelled chassis "Hummel". Not only the German forces but also Finland ("150 H/40") and Italy ("Obice da 149/28") used this weapon: after 1945 weapons of this type surfaced in the arsenals of Albania, Bulgaria, Portugal, Czechoslovakia and some South American countries and, somewhat modified, saw long service.

A 15-cm SFH 18 in a barracks. Notice the absence of the all-rubber tyres. (WKA)

A 15-cm sFH 18 under tow by an Sd.Kfz.7. (WKA)

15-cm schwere Feldhaubitze 36

Because of the great weight of the sFH 18, Krupp and Rheinmetall received orders from the Army Weapons department in 1935 to develop a lighter field howitzer with the same calibre for horse-drawn artillery units. The Rheinmetall design accepted in 1938 resembled the sFH 18 with its spreading tail chassis and all-rubber tyres, but had a shorter barrel. Most of the chassis and wheels were of light metal. The weapon was almost two tonnes lighter than the sFH 18 and its weight ready to fire was only 3280 kg.

Prototype of the 15-cm sFH 36 in firing position (above) and on limber for tow (below) (NARA)

As of necessity, the "sFH 36" was a much less solid design than the sFH 18 so that despite the use of a muzzle brake only a lesser propellant charge could be used, limiting the maxium range to 12,300 metres. Nevertheless small scale production was begun in 1939 but halted in 1942 because of the shortage of light metal alloys which became scarcer as the war went on and were given priority for aircraft production.

Type:	Heavy field howitzer
Calibre:	149 mm:
Barrel length:	3555 mm (L/23.7)
Weight for transport:	3500 kg
Weight, firing position:	3280 kg
Muzzle velocity:	485 m/sec
Weight of shell:	43.5 kg (HE)
Traverse:	56°
Elevation range:	-1°/+43°
Maximum range:	12,300 m
Rate of fire:	4 rounds(min
Manufacturer:	Rheinmetall, Düsseldorf

15-cm schwere Feldhaubitze 40

As a counter-weight design to the very light "sFH 36", in 1938 the Army Weapons Department asked for a howitzer with longer range than the sFH 18. In 1941 Krupp and Rheinmetall presented two prototypes designated "sFH 40" both intended for motor traction with longer barrels (L/32.5) and a larger load chamber (9.85 l instead of 7.22 l). The maximum range at 15.4 kilometres was greater by 2075 metres. In addition the elevation had been greatly increased so that the howitzer could fire up to +70° in the upper register. Lack of capacity prevented series production of the sFH 40; in 1942 therefore as an emergency solution the barrel with muzzle brake of the Krupp sFH 40 was set on a modified sFH 18 carriage. This weapon was designated "sFH 18/40" (then later "sFH 42") and 46 examples built. As compared to the sFH 18, accuracy in the short and medium ranges was inferior, and since the Army Weapons Department now wanted a totally new development with 360° traverse and a large elevation, work on the design was terminated.

Type:	Heavy field howitzer
Calibre:	149 mm
Barrel length:	4875 mm (L/32.5)
Weight for transport:	6200 kg
Weight, firing position:	5402 kg
Muzzle velocity:	595 m/sec
Weight of shell:	43.5 kg (HE)
Traverse:	56°
Elevation range:	0°/+70°
Maximum range:	15,400 m
Rate of fire:	4 rounds/min
Manufacturer:	Krupp, Essen

Prototype of the 15-cm sFH 40 (WKA)

15-cm schwere Feldhaubitze 37(t)

Type:	Heavy field howitzer
Calibre:	149.1 mm
Barrel length:	3600 mm (L/24)
Weight for transport:	5730 kg
Weight, firing position:	5200 kg
Muzzle velocity:	580 m/sec
Weight of shell:	42 kg (HE)
Traverse:	45°
Elevation range:	–5°/+70°
Maximum range:	15,100 m
Manufacturer:	Skoda, Pilsen

Skoda had developed a series of heavy field howitzers (K-series) since the early 1930s culminating in the "K-4" or "15-cm hruba houfnice vz. 37" in 1937. This very modern design with massive spreading box tail and pneumatic tyres was meant only for motorized towing and proved superior to most other heavy field howitzers of the time. The weight for firing of the K-4 was about 300 kg lighter than the German sFH 18, the range around 1775 metres longer. When the Wehrmacht marched into Czechoslovakia in March 1938, only a few of these howitzers had been delivered, but they were enough to convince the Wehrmacht of their efficient design, and production of gun and ammunition continued at Skoda under German supervision until

the end of 1941. The howitzers now designated "15-cm sFH 37(t)" saw service during the French campaign but were deployed primarily in the Balkans and on the Eastern Front, remaining in commission until the capitulation. After 1941 some of these "sFH 37(t)" were handed over to Axis allies such as the Slovak Army.

15-cm sFH 37(t) firing in Greece, April 1941. (BA)

The production of the 15-cm sFH 37(t) continued at Skoda even after the German occupation of Czechoslovakia.

15-cm Kanone 16

The "15-cm Kanone 16" was developed by Krupp during the First World War and saw service in the German Army from 1917. The Wehrmacht also used guns of this type, mostly for coastal defence or training. It was a child of its time with box tail chassis, steel wheels and all-rubber tyres. The return spring and recoil suppression were in the cradle below the barrel. Transport ensued in two parts, for this purpose the barrel was removed from the carriage and towed on a special trailer. For short stretches however the gun could be towed intact. In 1941 as a stop-gap measure a number of K 16 barrels were inset into the 21-cm Mrs 18 chassis. These guns were then designated "15-cm K 16 in

Type:	Heavy field gun
Calibre:	149.3
Barrel length:	6410 mm (L/43)
Weight for transport:	17,372 kg (two loads)
Weight, firing position:	10,870 kg
Muzzle velocity:	757 m/sec
Weight of shell:	51.4 kg (HE)
Traverse:	8°
Elevation range:	–3°/+42°
Maximum range:	22 kms
Rate of fire:	3 rounds/min
Manufacturer:	Krupp, Essen

Mrs Laf". Some which had gone as reparations under the provisions of the Treaty of Versailles to Belgium (known there as "Canon de 150 L/43") were commissioned into the Wehrmacht in the summer of 1940 as "15-cm K 429(b)".

15-cm K 16 exhibited at Dayton/Virginia, USA. (Seth Gaines)

15-cm K16 under tow intact at a pre-war parade.

15-cm Kanone 18

Type:	Heavy field gun
Calibre:	149.1 mm
Barrel length:	8200 mm (L/55)
Weight for transport:	18,700 kg (two sections)
Weight, firing position:	12,460 kg
Muzzle velocity:	865 m/sec
Weight of shell:	43 kg (HE)
Traverse:	11°
Elevation range:	−2°/+43°
Maximum range:	24,825 m
Rate of fire:	2 rounds/min
Manufacturer:	Rheinmetall, Düsseldorf

In 1933 the Army Weapons Department awarded Rheinmetall a contract to develop a successor to the 15-cm K 16. It finally reached the forces in 1938. The "15-cm K 18" was transported in two parts, broken down into barrel and carriage, although for short stretches the weapon could be towed in one piece. To lighten the re-fitting of the gun the box tail carriage had drop ramps which served the crew as a work platform during the procedure. Below the chassis was a drop-plate type two-part baseplate which provided the gun with additional stability and made it possible to traverse the weapon through 360°. Despite these modern characteristics and a weight increase of 1590 kg, the ballistic performance was not much better than that of the proven 15-cm K 16, and the improvement in range was only 2825 m over the older model. The great weight and the need to transport the gun in two parts were disadvantages soon recognized. Production was halted in 1943 after only 100 units had been turned out, but the gun remained in service until 1945.

15-cm K 18 ready for towing at a roadside. (Collection Holger Erdmann).

A 15-cm K 18 with limber below the chassis tail ready to tow. As with the the armoured vehicles, the guns exhibited at the Aberdeen Proving Ground (Maryland/USA) are in a deplorable state. (Seth Gaines).

15-cm Kanone 39

This weapon was developed by Krupp at the end of the 1930s for Turkey, which required a combined field- and coastal defence gun. Therefore it had a conventional spreading tail which when closed could be set on a transportable, rotatable base plate for a traverse of 360°. The procedure to get the base plate into position took time and required much effort. For transport the cannon was broken down into three parts: barrel, chassis and baseplate. The ballistic performance was similar to that of the 15-cm K 18 even though for the Turkish contract the gun fired a new type of shell.

By the outbreak of war in September 1939 Krupp had delivered only two of these guns to Turkey before the Army Weapons Department confiscated all the remainder either complete or under construction.

Type:	Heavy field gun
Calibre:	149.1 mm
Barrel length:	8250 mm (L/55.3)
Weight for trasnport:	18,282 kg (three parts)
Weight, firing position:	12,186 kg
Muzzle velocity:	865 m/sec
Weight of shell:	43 kg (HE)
Traverse:	60° (carriage), 360° (baseplate)
Elevation range:	-3°/+45°
Maximum range:	24,825 m
Rate of fire:	2 rounds/min
Manufacturer:	Rheinmetall, Düsseldorf

These were designated from 1940 "15-cm K 39" and put into service, production continuing until 1942. The Wehrmacht received a total of 64 guns of this type and they remained in service until 1945.

Of the 15cm K 30 originally designed for Turkey, Rheinmetall built only 64 examples for the Wehrmacht. (WKA)

15-cm Schiffskanone C/28M in C/38

Type:	Heavy field gun
Calibre:	149.1 mm
Barrel length:	8291 mm (L/55)
Weight for transport:	26,163 kg
Weight, firing position:	19,761 kg
Muzzle velocity:	875 m/sec (HE)
Weight of shell:	45.3 kg (HE)
Traverse:	360°
Elevation range:	-7°30'/+47°30
Maximum range:	23,500 m
Rate of fire:	up to 2 rounds/min
Manufacturer:	Rheinmetall, Düsseldorf

The SK C/28 had originally been developed for the heavy armoured units and battleships of the Kriegsmarine. At the end of the 1930s the Kriegsmarine gave Rheinmetall orders to develop a land-based mobile coastal artillery version. This variant had a six-armed cross-chassis (Type C/38) enabling a 360° traverse, and a large inclined splinter shield. The weapon was designed for motorized transport and given at the front and rear of the chassis a four-wheeled trailer with torsion bar spring and pneumatic tyres. Besides the naval artillery role, from 1940 a number of Army units also received the gun. It could only fire naval ammunition, and this was not compatible with the 15-cm shells and casings the Army used. This led to logistical problems and it would appear that eventually the Army received only 45 of these guns. A few of the 15-cm SK C/28 barrels were used for the 21-cm Mrs 18 mortar and the 17-cm K 18.

the 15-cm SK C/28M in position for transport.

15-cm SK C/28M detached from its transport trailers.

15.2-cm Kanonenhaubitze 433/1(r)

Type:	Heavy field howitzer
Calibre:	152.4 mm
Barrel length:	4405 mm (L/29)
Weight for transport:	7930 kg
Weight, firing position:	7128 kg
Muzzle velocity:	655 m/sec (HE), 670 m/sec (concrete shell)
Weight of shell:	43.5 kg (HE), 40 kg (concrete shell)
Traverse:	58°
Elevation range:	-2°/+65°
Maximum range:	17,265 m
Rate of fire:	1 round/min
Manufacturer:	Soviet State factories

In the initial phase following the invasion of the USSR on 22 June 1941, German forces captured huge quantities of Soviet artillery. Amongst these were almost 1000 15.2-cm howitzers Model 1937 (also known as "ML-20"), and in much smaller numbers their predecessor, the Model 1934. The

Eastern Front, summer 1941, captured 15.2-cm heavy field howitzers M1937. In the foreground an NSU Wehrmacht motor cycle. (WKA)

Wehrmacht also captured large stocks of ammunition. The M 1937 version was designated "KH 433/1" by the Germans, the M 1934 "KH 433/2". Both were modern, powerful guns and were amongst the first proper gun-howitzers, i.e. they were suitable for direct fire with a straight trajectory and also for steep fire with sharply curving trajectory. Characteristic of the gun were the two "horns" either side of the barrel, the coil-springs to equalize the barrel weight and the large multi-slit muzzle brake. The efficient "KH 433/1" was highly thought of throughout the Wehrmacht and was used on both the Eastern and Western Fronts. When the stocks of captured ammunition ran out at the beginning of 1943, a passable copy was manufactured in Germany. The Wehrmacht used the Russian 15.2-cm guns until the end of the war.

15.2-cm heavy field howitzer 433/1(r) at the Atlantic Wall.

15.2-cm heavy field howitzer 433/1(r) ready for transport with retracted barrel.

15.5-cm Kanone 418(f)

Type:	Heavy field gun
Calibre:	155 mm
Barrel length:	5915 mm (L/38.2)
Weight for transport:	11,700 kg
Weight, firing position:	10,750 kg
Muzzle velocity:	735 m/sec
Weight of shell:	43 kg (HE)
Traverse:	60°
Elevation range:	0°/+35°
Maximum range:	19,500 m
Rate of fire:	1-2 rounds/min
Manufacturer:	Not known

Amongst the best guns to fall into the hands of German forces after the fall of France in June 1940 were the 15.5-cm cannons of the type "GPF" from the First World War. Colonel L.J.F. Filloux designed this modern cannon with high muzzle velocity (Grand Puissance) from which the GPF tag came (Grand Puissance, Filloux). From 1917 it was the standard weapon of the French heavy artillery and in 1940 there were still 449 of them in service. The Wehrmacht took over most of these guns as "15.5-cm Kanone 418(f)". The variant, GPF-CA, Wehrmacht designation "15.5-cm K 417(f)" was practically similar in form but fired a modified ammunition. The GPF-T, Wehrmacht tag "15.5-cm K 419(f)", had a modern carriage with six pneumatic tyres. The tally of guns seized is not certain, but they were much liked by the Wehrmacht. In addition the Germans captured gigantic quantities of ammunition, more than 1.7 million rounds of HE and over 154,000 rounds of gas shells. Between 1943 and 1945 another 1.35 million shells were replicated in Germany. Guns of the type

GPF served with the German artillery on the Eastern Front, in North Africa and at the Atlantic Wall.

France, June 1940. A 15.5-cm Kanone GPF abandoned by French troops.

17-cm Kanone 18 in Mörser Lafette

Type:	Heavy cannon
Calibre:	172.5 mm
Barrel length:	8530 mm (L/49.4)
Weight for transport:	23,375 kg (two parts)
Weight, firing position:	17,510 kg
Muzzle velocity:	925 m/sec
Weight of shell:	68 kg (HE), 71 kg (AP)
Traverse:	16° (carriage), 360° (firing platform)
Elevation range:	0°/+50°
Maximum range:	29,600 m
Rate of fire:	1-2 rounds(min
Manufacturer:	Krupp, Essen; Hanomag, Hannover

The "17-cm K 18" resulted from an Army demand for a gun with very long range. Krupp suggested developing a new barrel to fit the "21-cm Mörser 18" already in service. On this carriage the barrel not only moved along the cradle, but back from the upper to the lower chassis. Both movements were suppressed by a hydro-pneumatic system. Together with a shooting platform which could be lowered, the combination proved remarkably stable and quiet with above-average accuracy and range. The gun was introduced in 1941, but was so heavy that transporting it intact over long stretches proved impossible. Therefore a purpose-built waggon was made for the barrel. The labour involved in putting the gun back together (despite all of Krupp's innovations to facilitate the process) was time-consuming. Nevertheless the gun was a sought-after prize for the Allies. By 1945 because of the difficulties in manufacture, only 338 had been built.

17-cm K18 in field possession, Italy, February 1944. (BA)

21-cm Mörser 16

The German Army had the original version of this particular mortar by 1910. In 1916 a modified version appeared with longer barrel, splinter shield and other refinements. Both guns were massive with box tail chassis and steel rims often fitted with wheel-belts to prevent the weapon sinking down in swampy ground. Two teams of horses were needed to transport it in two sections. The recoil brake was in an unusual position above the barrel. Those guns taken over by the Reichswehr at the end of the First World War were so modified during the 1930s that only the shield had to be removed for motorized towage. Additionally there were given new steel disc wheels with all-rubber tyres.

On 1 September 1939 the Army had 28 of these guns in action, and then they were gradually replaced in stages by the 21-cm Mrs 18 and passed to units in training or at the rear. Although the

Side profile of the Mrs 16.

Type:	Heavy mortar
Calibre:	211 mm
Barrel length:	3063 mm (L/14.6) Weight, firing position: 9220 kg
Weight, firing position:	9220 kg
Muzzle velocity:	393 m/sec (HE)
Weight of shell:	113 kg (HE), 121.4 kg (concrete shell)
Traverse:	4°
Elevation range:	–6°/+70°
Maximum range:	11,100 m
Rate of fire:	1–2 rounds/min
Manufacturer:	Krupp, Essen

After the end of the First World War Sweden had obtained a dozen of these guns from Germany, and they remained in service until the 1950s. Four of these were sold to Finland during the 1939-1940 Winter War against the Soviets.

The Finnish mortars did not enter service however until after Finland entered the war alongside the Reich against the Russians. The last weapons of this type were not scrapped in Finland until the late 1960s.

113 kg HE or 121.4 kg concrete shells were still effective, the weapon was obsolete and the range no longer acceptable. Along with the tag "Mrs 16" the gun is often known as the "21-cm long mortar".

Side profile of the Mrs 16.

21-cm Mörser 18

This gun was the successor to the obsolete "21-cm Mrs 16". As an innovation the Mrs 18 was given a chassis with double recoil track to enhance stability and accuracy. The principal difference to the "17-cm K 18" chassis was the barrel elevation to +70°. The Mrs 18 was a very heavy gun which had to be separated into two parts for transport. Despite its title as "mortar" it was better described as a field-howitzer: besides HE it fired special concrete shells against fortifications. Production of the "Mrs 18" began at Krupp in 1939 and by the outbreak of war there were 27 units operational. Another 460 followed by mid-1942 when production was halted. The reason for termination was that the 17-cm K 18

21-cm Mrs 18 on the coast of Northern Norway, 1943. (BA)

21-cm Kanone 38

The "21-cm K 38" was manufactured at Krupp in 1938 as a possible successor to the "21-cm Mrs 18" and used a further development of the double recoil suppression system: in this case the entire carriage ran back with the exception of the ground plate and chassis bed. This enhanced stability when firing. Four anchorage stakes driven into the ground prevented the ground plate moving when the gun fired. As with the Mrs 18, the K38 was also transported in two parts, the well thought-out design enabling the chassis to be lowered or raised without a crane or other devices.

Although the Army Weapons Department had ordered fifteen of these guns in 1940, production lagged and by 1943 when they came out only eight were delivered. One of them went by U-boat to Japan. The gun was outstanding and one of the best designs of its time, but the Army Weapons Department found the calibre unsuitable and cancelled the contract for the remaining seven units. Instead it requested the building of 24-cm cannons.

Type:	Heavy mortar
Calibre:	210.9 mm
Barrel length:	6510 mm (L/31)
Weight for transport:	22,700 kg (two loads)
Weight, firing position:	16,700 kg
Muzzle velocity:	565 m/sec
Weight of shell:	113 kg (HE) 121.4° (concrete shell)
Traverse:	16° (gun carriage) 360° (baseplate)
Elevation range:	0°/+70°
Maximum range:	18,700 m
Rate of fire:	1 round/min
Manufacturer:	Krupp, Essen

had almost twice the range. In 1941 (together with the 17-cm K 8) eight 15-cm barrels from naval stocks were fitted on Mrs 18 chassis, which were then designated "15-cm SK C/28 in Mrs Laf" (Mrs Laf-mortar chassis). Later they were replace by 17-cm barrels.

21-cm Mrs 18 with maximum barrel elevation. (WKA)

Type:	Heavy cannon
Calibre:	210.9 mm
Barrel length:	11,620 mm (L/55)
Weight for transport:	34,825 kg (two loads)
Weight, firing position:	16,700 kg
Muzzle velocity:	905 m/sec
Weight of shell:	120 kg (HE)
Traverse:	18° (gun carriage) 360° (baseplate)
Elevation range:	0°/+50°
Maximum range:	33,900 m
Rate of fire:	1 round/min
Manufacturer:	Krupp, Essen

Despite the efficiency of the 21-cm K 38, only eight models were built by 1943. (US Army)

21-cm Kanone 39

This cannon was originally developed by Skoda for Turkey under the designation "K 52". Only two were delivered before the occupation of Czechoslovakia by the Wehrmacht. Those guns still building were seized by the Germans and finished for their own purposes. The German "21-cm K 39" had a lower chassis which could revolve 360° resting on a groundplate set into the ground. Four foldable outrigger arms stabilized the gun. As three vehicles were needed to transport the parts (barrel, chassis and groundplate), setting up the gun was very time-consuming. In the course of the war various improvements were made to the basic design. While the "K39/40" underwent small-scale changes, the K39/41 was given a muzzle brake and with increased propellant had a range of 34 kilometres. All three versions were used primarily for coastal defence in France and Norway but also as

siege artillery on the Eastern Front, e.g. at Odessa, Sebastopol and Leningrad. Although inferior technically to the "21-cm K 38", a total of sixty guns of this type had been built by 1944.

Type:	Heavy cannon
Calibre:	210 mm
Barrel length:	10,766 mm (L/51.2), with muzzle brake 11,462 mm
Weight for transport:	59,100 kg (three loads)
Weight, firing position:	39,800 kg
Muzzle velocity:	800 m/sec
Weight of shell:	135 kg (HE)
Traverse:	360° (baseplate)
Elevation range:	-4°/+45°
Maximum range:	33,000 m
Rate of fire:	3 rounds every 2 mins
Manufacturer:	Skoda Works, Pilsen.

Side profile of the 21-cm K39 and its installation.
(Vincent Bourguignon)

US troops after the capture of the Crisbecq batgtery near Saint-Marcouf/Normady on 12 June 1944. The battery had three 21-cm K 39. (NARA)

24-cm Haubitze 39

This gun was the sister to the "21-cm K 39" and shared with it the same transporter and gun carriage. As with the K 39, installation was a lengthy business lasting six to eight hours since the ground plate had to be dug in first. Skoda had also designed this howitzer for export to Turkey, and in common with the K 52 only two were delivered before March 1939. The Germans seized the remainder and completed

Type:	Heavy howitzer
Calibre:	240 mm
Barrel length:	6756 mm (L/28)
Weight for transport:	42,900 kg (three loads)
Weight, firing position:	29 tonnes
Muzzle velocity:	597 m/sec
Weight of shell:	166 kg (HE)
Traverse:	360° (baseplate)
Elevation range:	-4°/+70°
Maximum range:	18,150 m
Rate of fire:	1 round every 2 mins
Manufacturer:	Skoda Works, Pilsen

As the 21-cm K 39, the 24-cm H 39 was often installed at fixed positions on the Atlantic Wall because of the time required to position it. (US Army)

them for their own account. In 1942 the design was simplified for war production and, as according to source, given a muzzle brake and redesignated "24-cm Haubitze 39/40". First operational presence occurred during the Western campaign in May/June 1940 but it is not clear whether the howitzers actually fired. Skoda built 18 howitzers of this type for the Germans. They were used primarily for coastal defence and on the Eastern Front.

Troops of 30th Div/US Army examine the upper carriage of a 24-cm H 39, abandoned near Wesel during the German retreat, 19 March 1945. (NARA)

24-cm Kanone 3

Type:	Heavy cannon
Calibre:	238 mm
Barrel length:	13,104 mm (L/54.6)
Weight for transport:	84,636 kg (six loads)
Weight, firing position:	54 tonnes
Muzzle velocity:	970 m/sec
Weight of shell:	152.3 kg (HE)
Traverse:	6° (carriage) 360° (baseplate)
Elevation range:	–1°/+56°
Maximum range:	37,500 m
Rate of fire:	One shell every three minutes
Manufacturer:	Rheinmetall, Düsseldorf and Krupp, Essen

In 1937 the 24-cm Kanone L/46 designed by Krupp was received by the forces. Its range was only 32 kilometres and the structure very complicated for which reason it was considered unsatisfactory and very few were made. Rheinmetall had begun with the development of an improved successor, the "24-cm K 3". The weapon itself had no particular specialities and the chassis used the double recoil system known from the Mrs 18. Because of its great weight the gun had to be transported in six loads (barrel, breech, cradle, upper chassis, ground plate and an electrical generator) but had been designed for re-assembly without a crane, cable winches fitted to gun and transporters being used instead. The first of these 24-cm guns was delivered in 1938; four were in service at the outbreak of war. Although the Army Weapons Department issued a contract for forty, by 1944 only fourteen had been built, eight by Rheinmetall and six by Krupp. During the war various methods were tried out to increase the range. Together with changes to the barrel rifling, tests were held with sabot shells (shell fitted with a device to enable the use of a projectile smaller than the bore diameter) and with smooth-bore and conical barrels. An experimental barrel with calibre reducing from 24-cm to 21-cm provided a muzzle velocity of 1113 m/sec and a range of 51.5-cm, but tungsten-core ammunition was necessary which after 1942 was no longer available.

Although only fourteen 24-cm K 3 were built, the type is one of the best known of the Wehrmacht's heavy guns.

28-cm Haubitze L/12

This weapon originated in the early 20th century and was originally developed at Krupp as a coastal mortar to lay steep trajectory fire on enemy armoured ships. The purpose was to avoid the heavily armoured hull and provide plunging fire into the weakly armoured decking. The introduction of long-range ships' guns soon made this mortar obsolete for its poor range. Nevertheless after 1919 the Reichswehr took charge of a number, these being reactivated at the outbreak of the Second World War. Main reason was the Wehrmacht's lack of heavy guns, causing the surviving 28-cm howitzers to be brought out from the depots to serve as siege artillery. The Army appears to have used nineteen of this type. The antiquity of the howitzer was clearly seen from its profile. The recoil forces were not fully absorbed by a modern recoil system although a portion of them were absorbed by the barrel cradle running back along a slightly upwards-inclined slope on the upper chassis. The upper chassis could be traversed 360° on a wooden platform.

A 28-cm Haubitze L/12 firing during the siege of Sevastopol, 1942.

Side profile of the 28-cm Haubitze L/12, notice the ammunition crane for the 350 kg shell. (Vincent Bourguignon).

Type:	Heavy howitzer
Calibre:	283 mm
Barrel length:	3396 mm (L/112)
Weight, firing position:	37 tonnes
Muzzle velocity:	379 m/sec
Weight of shell:	350 kg (HE)
Traverse:	360°
Elevation range:	0°/+65°
Maximum range:	11,400 m
Rate of fire:	1 round/min
Manufacturer:	Krupp, Essen

The howitzer was reduced to four parts for transport (barrel, cradle, chassis and wooden bedding). To instal the gun first a pit had to be dug for the bed before the howitzer could be re-assembled. Therefore the weapon was only used as a siege gun, as for example in 1942 for the siege of Sebastopol and to put down the Warsaw uprising in 1944.

30.5-cm Mörser(t)

Of the forty-three guns of calibre 24-cm or over which the Wehrmacht had available in May 1940, twenty-three came from the stocks of the former Austro-Hungarian Army. In 1906 Skoda had started development on a heavy siege gun, introduced into the Austro-Hungarian Army in 1911. In 1916 an improved model of the M.1911 followed with changed upper chassis, longer barrel and greater range, this being the "30.5-cm Mörser M.16". Both versions had a massive box bedding and were transported in three loads. For this purpose Ferdinand Porsche at Austro-Daimler developed special road tugs with petrol-electric propulsion. Both types of mortar were taken subsequently by the

Type:	heavy mortar
Calibre:	305 mm
Barrel length:	3660 mm (L/12)
Weight for transport:	35.5 tonnes
Weight, firing position:	23.1 tonnes
Muzzle velocity:	448 m/sec
Weight of shell:	300 kg (HE)
Traverse:	360°
Elevation range:	-4°/+75°
Maximum range:	12.3 kms
Rate of fire:	1 round every 5 mins
Manufacturer:	Skoda, Pilsen

successor States to the Danube monarchy, amongst them Hungary, Yugoslavia, Czechoslovakia and of course Austria. In 1938/1939 the Wehrmacht took possession of one Mörser M.16 from Austria and

The 30.5-cm Mörser M16 operational with the Czechoslovak Army pre-war.

seventeen from Czechoslovakia and installed them as siege guns in Poland and France under the designation "30.5-cm Mörser(t)". In 1941 five more guns, "30.5-cm Mörser(j)", came from Yugoslavia and were operational on the Eastern Front together with other guns of the type. A few 30.5-cm Mörser M.11 captured in Yugoslavia and used there as coastal artillery were designated "30.5-cm Mörser 639(j)".

30.5-cm Mörser(t) in action.

One of the 30.5-cm mortars captured by US forces at the war's end ready to transport. To the right the barrel, left the upper chassis. This is the barrel on its transporter waggon. (NARA)

35.5-cm Haubitze M 1

Type:	Heavy howitzer
Calibre:	355.6 mm
Barrel length:	10,165 mm (L/28.9
Weight for transport:	123.5 tonnes (six loads)
Weight, firing position:	78 tonnes
Muzzle velocity:	575 m/sec
Weight of shell:	575 kg (concrete shells)
Traverse:	6° (chassis), 360° ground plate
Elevation range:	+45°/+75°
Maximum range:	20,850 m
Rate of fire:	1 riund every 4 minutes
Manufacturer:	Rheinmetall, Dusseldorf

The design of this heavy gun began at Rheinmetall in 1936, the first example being delivered in 1939. The "35.5-cm H M 1" bore some similarities to the "24-cm K 23", including the double recoil system and 360° traverse on a ground plate. Six 18-tonne tractors (Sd.Kfz 9) were used to tow the dismantled gun for transport, plus a seventh Sd.Kfz 9 to haul the crane with electric drive required to position the massive howitzer. The generator for this latter Sd.Kfz 9 had its own tractor and also supplied the current for the elevation and traverse machinery of the weapon. The howitzer fired only one kind of ammunition, a concrete shell weighing 575-kg with an HE charge of only 7.9 kg which with the maximum propellant had a range of 20,850 metres. The so-called "Röchling Concrete Shell" of 925 kg which could go through 4 metres of concrete did not pass the trial stage. After being deployed in the Western campaign in 1940, used against the Belgian forts, these howitzers were only in action again in the East, where they were used to besiege Sebastopol and Leningrad and put down the Warsaw uprising. Between 1939 and 1944, Rheinmetall turned out eight of them.

A 35.5-cm M1 being manhandled into position. (BA)

42-cm Gamma-Mörser

Type:	Heavy mortar
Calibre:	420 mm
Barrel length:	6723 mm (L/16)
Weight for transport:	327.5 tonnes (ten loads)
Weight, firing position:	140 tonnes
Muzzle velocity:	452 m/sec
Weight of shell:	1003 kg (concrete shell)
Traverse:	45°
Elevation range:	+42°/+75°
Maximum range:	14.2 kms
Rate of fire:	1 round every 8 mins
Manufacturer:	Krupp, Essen

The design of this siege howitzer (originally designated "42-cm Mörser L/16" or "gamma-Mörser") originated in 1906. As according to the source consulted, between 1910 and 1918 Krupp delivered ten or twelve of them. Although the Treaty of Versailles forbade the possession by Germany of heavy artillery, one howitzer at the Meppen firing grounds escaped scrapping by being in a dismantled condition and was reactivated in the mid-1930s. It served at first as a test gun for concrete shells, but was later used operationally, amongst other places, at the Maginot Line in 1940, Sebastopol in 1942 and to put down the Warsaw uprising in 1944.

The gamma-Mörser was a massive weapon of 140 tonnes and had to be transported by rail. If the gun was dismantled and loaded on ten railway waggons, the total mass of weapon, fixtures (bedding materials, crane) and transport waggon came to 327 tonnes. To ready it in position for firing first a great pit had to be dug for the bedding which (depending on the kind of ground selected) would take between two and five days. Because the breech was 3.4 metres high, an electrically driven ammunition lift was needed to convey the concrete shells of 1003 kg. The "gamma-Mörser" is not to be confused with "Big Bertha", also of 42 cm calibre but fired from a wheeled chassis.

The Wehrmacht was able to use only this single 42-cm Gamma-Mörser which escaped being scrapped stored in sections on the Meppen firing grounds. (WKA)

42-cm Haubitze(t)

This heavy siege gun is another example of the numerous former Czech artillery pieces to be found in the Wehrmacht arsenal. The origins of the gun go back to 1909-10 when Skoda designed the "42-cm Küstenhaubitze M.14" for the Austro-Hungarian Army as a fixed installation to defend the port of Pola. In the First World War the design was modified for transport in six parts on special Daimler petrol-electric tractors. An improvement to the Model M.17

Type:	Heavy howitzer
Calibre:	420 mm
Barrel length:	6290 mm (L/15)
Weight for transport:	160 tonnes (four loads)
Weight for firing:	105 tonnes
Muzzle velocity:	435 m/sec (HE)
Weight of shell:	1020 kg (HE)
Traverse:	360°
Elevation range:	+40°/+71°
Maximum range:	14,600 m
Rate of fire:	1 round every five minutes
Manufacturer:	Skoda Works, Pilsen

The 42-cm howitzer(t) was a Skoda design from the First World War. Along with this gun the Wehrmacht had a number of other former Czech steep-trajectory guns of 21 and 24-cm calibre.

resulted in transport in only four parts. Nevertheless the installation procedure was time-consuming, for a pit had to be excavated for the bedding on which the chassis could swivel through 360°. This version was never operational in the Great War, but was used afterwards by the Czech Army ("42-cm houfnice vx. 17") and seized by the Wehrmacht in March 1939. At least one of these heavy howitzers was at the bombardment of the Maginot Line on the Franco-German border in 1940 and later on the Eastern Front, amongst other places at the siege of Leningrad, and also at Sebastopol where 192 of its 1020 kg heavy shells were fired at the fortifications.

42-cm Haubitze(t) elevated to fire in the upper register. (WKA)

42-cm Haubitze(t) at the siege of Sebastopol, June–July 1942. (WKA)

60-cm Mörser "Karl Gerät"

The first planning for this weapon began in 1935/36. The Army Weapons Department declined the first suggested version of a bedded gun similar to the "gamma-Mörser" and wanted a type capable of quicker installation. In 1937 therefore Rheinmetall designed a self-propelled chassis with caterpillar tracks and a 580-hp DB engine. The heavy weight made it necessary to dis-assemble the gun into three parts for long hauls or to suspend it between two special railway waggons. Before firing the body was lowered hydraulically to the ground in order to better absorb the enormous recoil forces. At first all six SP-chassis received a 60-cm mortar ("Gerät 40"). After the barrels were worn down, 54-cm mortars L/13 replaced them ("Gerät 41"), these could fire a heavy

Type:	Heavy mortar
Calibre:	600 mm
Barrel length:	5070 mm (L/8.5)
Weight for transport:	120 tonnes (on caterpillar tracks)
Weight, firing position:	120 tonnes
Length:	11,150 mm
Muzzle velocity:	279 m/sec (HE), 222 m/sec (concrete shell)
Weight of shell:	1700 kg (HE), 2180 kg (concrete shell)
Traverse:	5°
Elevation range:	0°/+70°
Maximum range:	6580 m (HE), 4320 m (concrete shell)
Rate of fire:	1 round every 8 mins
Manufacturer:	Rheinmetall, Düsseldorf

concrete shell of 1580 kg up to 10.5 kilometres. A seventh, fitted at the works with the 54-cm mortar, was never in action. Operations ensued principally

The six 60-cm mortars built were named after the Germanic gods/goddesses Thor, Freya, Ziu, Loki, and also Adam and Eve ("Eva"). "Adam" can be seen today in the tank museum at Kubinka, Russia. Behind to the left the rear of an ammunition panzer IV can be seen. The body of the mortar is lowered. (NARA)

on the Eastern Front, thus for example in 1941 at Brest-Litovsk, in 1942 at Sebastopol and Warsaw in 1944. Each of the SP-chassis had two special ammunition carriers on a Pz.Mk.IV base with cranes for handling the shells up to 2180 kg in weight. The name "Karl Gerät" comes from artillery general Karl Becker who was involved in the development.

Mortar "Adam", Schwere Artillerie Abtg. 833/11.Armee, at the siege of Sebastopol, June-July 1942. (Vincent Bourguignon).

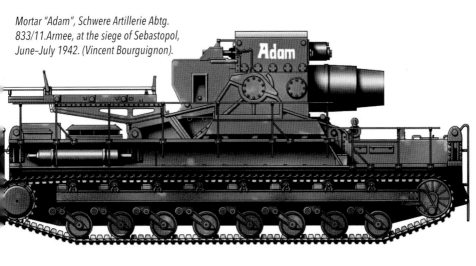

For long hauls the chassis could be suspended between two special railway bogies. (NARA)